# EVERY LEADER IS
## AN
# ARTIST

# EVERY LEADER IS
## AN
# ARTIST

---

## HOW THE WORLD'S GREATEST
## ARTISTS CAN MAKE YOU
## A MORE CREATIVE LEADER

MICHAEL O'MALLEY AND WILLIAM F. BAKER

NEW YORK   CHICAGO   SAN FRANCISCO
LISBON   LONDON   MADRID   MEXICO CITY   MILAN
NEW DELHI   SAN JUAN   SEOUL   SINGAPORE
SYDNEY   TORONTO

The *McGraw·Hill* Companies

1 2 3 4 5 6 7 8 9 10   DOC/DOC   1 9 8 7 6 5 4 3 2

ISBN 978-0-07-177857-2
MHID        0-07-177857-8

e-ISBN 978-0-07-177858-9
e-MHID        0-07-177858-6


**Library of Congress Cataloging-in-Publication Data**

O'Malley, Michael, 1954-
    Every leader is an artist : how the world's greatest artists can make you a more creative leader / by Michael O'Malley and William Baker.—1st ed.
        p. cm.
    ISBN-13: 978-0-07-177857-2 (alk. paper)
    ISBN-10: 0-07-177857-8 (alk. paper)
    1. Leadership.    I. Baker, William.    II. Title.
    HD57.7.0443    2012
    658.4'092—dc23                                                    2012009350

McGraw-Hill books are available at special quantity discounts to use as premiums and sales promotions or for use in corporate training programs. To contact a representative, please e-mail us at bulksales@mcgraw-hill.com.

This book is printed on acid-free paper.

To Alfred Moses, Gene Ludwig, Mark Jacobsen, and our many friends at Promontory Financial Group—where quality leadership is alive and well.

# Contents

# Foreword

There is no dearth of books on leadership. The topic captivates attention and inspires thoughts of self-aggrandizement as much as commitments to self-sacrifice. So many of us are seeking either the definitive formula to apply to our own circumstances or the iconic human to emulate. Yet deep in our psyches, we know that human behavior would be difficult to reduce to a formula, and examples of great leaders are hard to copy while preserving the same effect that induced others to call them great in the first place.

And were those designated leaders really so great? What was so special about Catherine or Alexander, for example? Each wears the moniker of "great" in history books. Were their respective distinctions matters of circumstance, or were their successors simply lacking certain special qualities that Catherine and Alexander each had in ample supply?

Management has often been viewed as a combination of science and art. But when we assert that, what do we mean by *art*? Are we thinking of the product of a painter, a composer, a writer, a sculptor? Perhaps, if set in an appropriate context and if one allows for a degree of metaphor. Yet it may be that the art in management is not at all metaphorical.

Michael O'Malley and William Baker present a highly readable and thoughtful treatment of the leader as artist. They begin with first principles, the most important of which is that leadership is a state of mind. They then lead us through what it means to be an artist in the context of management. Focus, skill, form, representation, and imagination are hallmarks of the making of art and, as we come to appreciate, the making of a leader in a management setting.

Not only do O'Malley and Baker help us to understand what art is and how it relates to leadership, they explain its outcomes (engagement and pleasure as enrichment). They also explain the significance of art and leadership for society, how it adapts to and reflects elements of changing contexts.

As a business school dean, I can certainly see how *Every Leader Is an Artist* can provoke a rethinking of business, its purpose, and its value to society. Chapter 14 may be the kind of indictment of MBA programs that I would rather not read, but I know I need to. By simply asking ourselves where art is in business, we might discover more leaders in places and positions where we have not looked before. If business schools could condition their communities to seek consciously for art in the context of business, then I think that leaders in business would respect themselves more and see their occupation more genuinely as a profession. Business schools would do well to take seriously the message and the insights of this book.

—David A. Gautschi, PhD,
Dean of the Graduate School of Business Administration,
Fordham University

# Acknowledgments

We have many to thank for their helpful suggestions on various iterations of the manuscript. Collectively, they fixed our grammatical errors and oversights, refined our aesthetic arguments, enlarged our appreciation of certain artists, and provided new insights into leadership. In alphabetical order, these commentators were Julie Adams, Amnon Bergerbest, Jaya Aninda Chatterjee, Ellen de Saint Phalle, Catherine Goetschel, Karen Hayward, Charles Karelis, Christopher Miller, and Kathryn O'Malley. Naturally, we alone are responsible for all that is said in this, the final version, of the manuscript.

We also are indebted to our agent, Susan Ginsburg of Writers House, who saw the promise in this project and who provided guidance throughout the development and production of the work. We also are grateful to the talented people at McGraw-Hill who were extremely proactive, insightful, and encouraging throughout the process. In particular, we would like to extend special thanks to our editors, Leila Porteous and Knox Huston, and to our editing supervisor, Janice Race, for their timely and incisive guidance and suggestions.

Finally, we appreciate the tolerance of our respective families, who were forced to endure stacks of papers, strange working hours, the highs and lows of writing, and the diminution of our free time over an extended period. Thank you.

# EVERY LEADER IS
## AN
# ARTIST

# Introduction

The business press routinely selects the top leaders of industry as part of its year-end review. These ritualistic roundups put the exclamation point on the year's corporate news by calling out headliner executives whose companies' growth surpassed expectations and who successfully managed their companies' public personas as customer friendly, socially responsible, and ethically upright. It is entertaining reading, but if you, like us, have been through enough of these annual cycles, you know that both the names of the executives and the companies they represent come and go. Exalted corporations are broken up, taken over, or go under. Celebrated leaders featured in books and magazines fade away or spectacularly flame out as miscreants, bunglers, con artists, or embezzlers, dragging their erstwhile healthy companies into the financial abyss. A casual retrospective easily illustrates the point. Bernard Ebbers, Dennis Kozlowski, Ken Lay, and Joseph Nacchio were revered executives before their legal troubles began. Yet these few merely personify corporate abuse. Hundreds of affable and beloved executives have been convicted of insider trading, falsifying records, bribing officials, scamming friends, and unlawfully padding their bank accounts. In all these instances, a hiring authority handed these people key cards to the executive suites. Hundreds of other executives, gala honorees cast as model citizens, have managed to enrich themselves while doing immeasurable damage to their companies and society within the letter of the law.

Nevertheless, we are only modestly bothered by the misplaced praise we heap on the undeserving and the corresponding neglect of the worthy. We know that some villains are mistaken as heroes and that some saints never make it onto the calendar—to paraphrase Erasmus. More disconcerting to us is the ease with which we accept determinations of greatness as true even though we know that some of the honorees are likely to be frauds. Would we as readily acquiesce to the press's assessments of superiority in other fields? For example, would the rankings of sports stars, politicians, movies, or rock groups go uncontested? We would anticipate a robust debate about each of these that would linger online for months. Yet when it comes to estimations of business leadership, there is a notable silence. It would be refreshing for once to see someone walk into a conference room and slam a copy of *Forbes* on the table and rhetorically ask, "Did you see this? Can you believe they named this guy a great leader?" Instead, we find a curious absence of protest, and we wonder why.

It can't be that businesspeople care less about business than enthusiasts in other disciplines. Plenty of people are consumed by business and feast on the extensive media fare that caters to their interests. We can easily dismiss other possible explanations as well. Don't have the time to bother? Everyone is pressed for time yet manages to find it when the issues are large enough for comment. Worried about reprisals for public statements, particularly condemnations? Many people lie outside the grasp of retaliation and can fearlessly render opinions. We seem to care enough and have plenty of opportunity to express ourselves but, nevertheless, leave corporate leadership alone.

We propose another explanation: we have neither a solid foundation of what leadership is nor a shared way to talk about it. The reason we don't openly debate the quality of corporate leadership is that we don't know how to. This claim may seem surprising given all that has been written about leadership.

However, as far as our understanding of leadership may have progressed, the anecdotal evidence suggests we still have a long way to go. We will let experience be our proof. First, for every corrupt official or slimy executive on the evening news, there are many others practicing their leadership craft on the fringes of legality and a multitude who are ineptly and meanly making life unbearable for others. Second, we have been unable to do anything about this state of affairs. We continually place the wrong or poorly equipped people into positions of leadership and hope for the best: indeed, many of those today who occupy positions of authority never actually aspired to those positions and were thrust into their new roles based on coincidence and time spent with their company. We nonchalantly or haphazardly assess their aptitude to lead, sometimes placing laurels on heads that should be shoved, metaphorically, into guillotines. We get it wrong so often that how could we possibly maintain that we know what we are doing?

There is no common formulation, method of development, or means of evaluation for leadership. Consultancies vie for corporate attention by offering unique brands of leadership and convincing buyers that, among the panoply of options, their approach is the best. These concoctions are made possible, and their restorative powers believable, by the absence of standards by which their theses may be measured. A simple thought experiment further illustrates the vagaries of leadership. Imagine asking a room full of executives for their definitions of leadership. Do you doubt that among these supposed experts you would get a room full of divergent replies? There would be some overlap to be sure, but it would be too slight to grasp. We would discover, instead, that we use the word *leadership* liberally to represent all kinds of relationships and accountabilities. We use the term to designate a position of authority, a rank within the hierarchy, a bundle of responsibilities, or a degree of programmatic oversight. *Leader* is a word that readily attaches to a great many individuals in a variety of circumstances. Nevertheless, despite ubiquitous references to leaders and leadership, we still have a poor idea about what constitutes true leadership and special difficulty identifying those elite few who excel at it.

Despite yeomen's efforts to pin down the idea of leadership, definitions remain either frustratingly vague or overly narrow. The pithy one-liners of shrink-wrapped wisdom lack that all-important ingredient of substance. Therefore, when someone states that leaders are dealers of hope, intentional influencers, or purposeful travelers who take us from where we are to where we have never been, we are entertained but unfulfilled: these are phrases that sound right but yield little practical direction. When the wonders of these clever sound bites wear off, those in search of genuine understanding are left stranded.

On the other hand, many descriptions of leadership are thoughtfully executed and clear, but they are incomplete because they address only certain aspects of leadership. In other words, each conception captures only a sliver of the whole. A sample of the varieties of leadership discussed in the social science literature includes transformational, transactional, visionary, charismatic, transcendent, authentic, servant, spiritual, shared, leader-member, path-goal, participatory, contingency, and situational. And there are more … many more. Some of these approaches focus on context, some on the leaders' traits, some on followers' attributes, some on results, some on processes, some on interpersonal dynamics, some on structure and rules, some on mental states and motives, some on observable behaviors, and so forth. If each of these were elevated to the status of a comprehensive theory intended to convey everything there is to be said about leadership, the result would be utter confusion. And that, in fact, is what we often get as discussions about leadership move back and forth across alternate ideas that address different aspects of what it means to lead. Just as at Babel, we are speaking different languages.

Ideally, we need a structured, agreed-upon set of criteria that meaningfully encompass most of what is meant by leadership that, in turn, could be used to inform our judgments about leadership. Evaluative discussions would then have the same feel as the deliberations of friends after a movie. The natural inclination of moviegoers is to share their experiences with one another, stating what they like and don't like about a film. These discussions follow predictable pathways. In making their assessments, members of the group grapple with the sorts of things that make movies good: plot, character development, special effects, set, music, costume design, script, and so on—and how each of these is woven together. These conversations are possible because everyone is working from the same set of assumptions, cultural norms, and frames of reference. In fact, we are frustrated by those who ignore the interpretive conventions and insist on having opinions for which they need no reasons to support.

When appraising leadership ability, then, our solution is to assemble a set of criteria that most everyone would agree is essential for leadership excellence, and use that set as our standard for evaluation.[1] With this book, we have done just that: produced the signal characteristics of leadership. We are not going to hedge on naming the criteria, but before we move the conversation in that direction, we want to mention the advantages of our approach and why we think it is the right one to take. First, it corresponds to our intuition about leadership that there is no one best or true form. We don't consider the criteria we present to be necessary *and* sufficient, meaning that it is possible to be a good leader in many different ways. There is no leadership template to which all leaders must conform in order to be considered good. Leadership is more open ended than that. Leaders will be better on certain criteria, and in particular ways, than on others, and they won't all be the same. We suggest that many words cannot be precisely or exclusively defined. Consider the meaning of a word such as *respect*. A host of descriptors can be used to circle the word but never quite pin it down for every use and circumstance. Leadership falls into the same camp of words—you are able to surround it with descriptive terminology of possible meanings without entirely being able to say what combination of phrases must be true under all conditions.

This bit of permissiveness regarding the criteria does not imply that leadership becomes whatever we want it to be. Instead, the criteria set limits as in the rules of a game. In baseball, there are many ways to turn a double play or advance runners, but those ways are fenced in by rules. The game doesn't become chaotic simply because the possibilities for what counts as a double play, for example, are open. In fact, the game is more interesting because of it. Similarly, the criteria for leadership operate as constraints, imposing limits on what will count toward leadership but not allowing us to make it up as we go along, either.

Second, our approach can accommodate changes in context and culture because the way we interpret the criteria may change with the times. Leadership is a creative discipline, and we need to give it some space. Leadership won't be viewed the same way at all times and in all places. If, for example, we said that technical proficiency, or skill, is one criterion for leadership, we might expect a leader from the early years of the twentieth century to have a firm grasp of the scientific method and time-motion techniques. These same expectations today would be considered old-fashioned, but does that give us license to retrospectively critique leaders of the past as hopelessly flawed? We don't think so. We would want to view the leaders in their context. Unless you care to argue that there is one unalterable version of leadership that persists for all time, there has to be some fluidity in how we think about leadership. Fixed definitions of leadership don't admit social or technological innovations, transitions in business and society, or modifications in our worldviews. Additionally, they don't allow us to slide our evaluations based on leaders' positions and levels of development. For example, our general inclination is to tone down the criticism for novices and say, "He's pretty good for a project manager," or "She shows a lot of promise," rather than hold the person to rigid standards that he or she cannot possibly meet. We don't expect the same performances from apprentices as we do from those who have been given ample time to mature. A set of standards with malleable understandings allows us to adjust our language to the circumstances.

Third, our approach allows us to use the same universal criteria for all kinds of leaders at all organizational levels—without having to create new categories or resort to fine and unnecessary distinctions. It doesn't matter if a person is a homemaker, chef, pilot, foreman, or executive. It doesn't matter how many people a person oversees and whether those people are skilled or unskilled, young or old, short or tall. It doesn't matter what else the person may be: organized, introverted, thrifty, or friendly. In order to be assessed as a leader, one must be measured against the criteria for leadership. Similarly, the supposed leader must be engaged in an activity that he or she thinks is leadership: that is, the person must be trying to do leadership as opposed to something else. Having said that, we can hear the echo of "I don't care what you call it as long as he's (she's) making money" ricocheting off corporation walls. But it does matter, because calling someone a leader (or alluding to oneself as a leader) invites a different kind of look—and a different set of behaviors—than someone who simply is out to make a buck personally and for the company. If all that matters, for example, is an individual's financial acumen and money-making ability, then that person should be evaluated strictly on those terms. The result may be that he or she is a financial guru and valuable corporate contributor, but nothing can be said about that person's leadership ability unless leadership is perceived as an organizational concern, and the person is held out as a leader and evaluated as such. Similarly, if the principal duty of an office manager is to mind the budget, then regardless of how many people are under his or her authority, the office manager cannot be considered a leader unless someone, anyone, thinks leading should be a fundamental aspect of the role of office manager. He or she may be a very good accountant and great budgetary overlord, but nothing more can be said unless the person is expected to be more than a super-accountant.

One of the reasons we have a leadership deficit in many of our organizations is because we don't expect more from those who have been given supervisory roles. We expect them to do their jobs, and not to be great leaders. Many companies can go years without mention of the word *leadership* in their hallways except in passing or theoretical conversations. We can think of only two reasons why leadership remains a foreign body in the workplace. First, leadership isn't seen as that important. The presumption is that improvements in leadership won't make a difference in how the company operates or advances its fortunes; if there is a pretense of interest, the superficial gesture is quickly revealed when leadership development is one of the first corporate programs to be cut during austere periods. Second, even if executives think that leadership is important, the fact that they do little about it suggests a belief that there is nothing that can be done—the company is blessed or stuck with the people they have, and while it is possible to make them better workers, it isn't possible to make them better leaders.

By contrast, the best companies, those known for developing leaders and sending their minions out into the world to populate the executive ranks of other companies, expect more from their people. We are thinking of companies with reputations for visible and rigorous leadership development programs and evaluative follow-through such as General Electric, Procter & Gamble, Southwest Airlines, Nestlé, and PepsiCo. At the risk of offending those who dedicated themselves to the creation of these programs, the active ingredients may not be contained in the programs themselves but in what they say about the kind of institution one wants. The programs are not placebos. The effects of these programs are real, except that they do their work by communicating a few key messages: that leadership matters, it carries a set of obligations that people conduct themselves in a particular manner, and it is a discipline unto itself that requires hard work to master.

We think leadership is a separate discipline. Regardless of whether the study of leadership rises to the status of a profession is immaterial. The more central point is that people accept their responsibilities as leaders and work at improving their performance in this domain. Leadership is a special form of art that takes time and persistence to master. In fact, in taking on the slippery questions of "What is leadership?" and "How do we know it when we have it?" it is helpful to think about leadership in precisely this way—as an art form.

The connections between leadership and art have been made many times over, usually as a way to single out certain properties of the arts that carry over to leadership, such as a jazz musician's ability to create through improvisation or a stage actor's ability to affect others through emotionally controlled performances. These are compelling ways to explore the role of spontaneity to creative activity and of presence to persuasion. The analogies are helpful because they enable greater insight into one practice by examining another. Nevertheless, they *are* analogies, and our plan is more ambitious. Our claim isn't that leadership is metaphorically an art, rather, that it *is* an art. It covers the same territory and can be viewed in the same light as the arts. It is helpful to think of the work of a leader as a work of art since the connection highlights the leader's very public mission and the need for both superior technical abilities and acute nontechnical sensitivities to pull it off well.

Therefore, our thesis is literal. The same traits that distinguish great artists from the mediocre distinguish exceptional leaders from the ordinary. It works. Both leadership and art are forms of expression that made the trip from antiquity to the present because both have been worth preserving in human societies—and not just for the functional advantages they afford but for all the reasons that make us human. Leaders and artists both give us perspective on our social condition, good or bad, and greater appreciation of our world, ourselves, and our choices. They challenge, excite, comfort, and motivate. They bring us closer together by providing a forum for shared experiences and forging a sense of community. Leadership and art animate social encounters and have the potential to change lives in ways that are as invigorating and real as if hit by a wave.

You, leaders, are artists: a realization that should overwhelm as well as humble. It underscores your public role and the risks involved. You are putting your work on display every day, and like an artist, you should know what it feels like to occupy such a perilously exposed space. Additionally, if you take the idea that you are an artist seriously, then you are bound to reflect anew on how you lead and what you might do differently to improve. Works of art are notoriously unfinished; just where one work stops the next begins—bolder, more intimate, more vibrant, more penetrating, more novel, and so on. Great artists always strive to be better artists, no matter how good they may be. In other words, leadership is something you work to perfect over time. It isn't something you wholly acquire with the receipt of a graduate degree or corporate title. Nor is leadership a skill that can be honed through osmosis—through passive observation and tenure. Excellence in any craft requires greater energy and dedication than that. Many academics and corporate insiders have voiced considerable dissatisfaction with the way we train our leaders today and with the quality of leadership. As a result, we rethink leadership education in Chapter 14 using artistic development as a partial guide.

Conventional art, of course, is not without its ambiguities and controversies, but it has some advantages as a lens for leadership. For one, it is a more tangible art form than leadership. Some art may have a limited life span (we're thinking of installation art or works that self-destruct), but you are still able to observe the art-making process and the outcomes of the work over a period of time, however abbreviated. The confinement of traditional arts makes them a convenient object of study and an instructive conceptual bridge to leadership.

Second, while people may disagree about the quality of a work of art, people generally talk about the same sorts of things when viewing art. Given varied tastes and experiences, some people may zero in on some features of the art more than others, but if pressed, the individual onlookers would produce a similar list of factors used to inform their judgments. Art critics would add a few more items that the public may have overlooked, but in the end, we would have an inclusive list of the criteria that govern the attitudes of most people toward art. That is the list we present below, and it applies to all arts, including the one we wish to address—leadership. The dozen attributes we provide represent the distinguishing characteristics of leadership: what separates great leadership from poor leadership, or from activities that would be difficult to classify as leadership at all. As we describe each of these throughout the book, it will become evident that many of the criteria correspond to elements of leadership discussed in the management literature, now reassembled in one place as essential features of leadership art.

There is no numeric scale to accompany the list or definitive cutoff that separates the good from the bad and ugly. We don't rate leadership from 1 to 100 for the same reason we don't quantify art: it can't be done. A point system could never capture the many ways leadership may be exhibited, nor could it appropriately summarize the strengths and weaknesses of a leader's work. Indeed, viewed in the context of an art form, assessing leadership in whole numbers seems crude. It feels expedient... and wrong. A person is more than this. The natural and better way to appraise the value of a leader is the same way we do it with a piece of art. We say it in words. We accumulate evidence over time and across people and form a consensus opinion that we express with evaluative language. On the positive side, for example, leadership may be described as inspiring, consistent, creative, unique, passionate, and engaging. Alternatively, leadership may be perceived as unpleasant, phony, inept, unfocused, and pedestrian. We gather and discuss reasons and summarize the results in terms more honest than a number.

These are our 12 criteria:

## Leadership Criteria

1. *Intent.* Makes an express commitment to achieve certain exceptional ends

2. *Focus.* Uses various verbal and nonverbal means to highlight certain features of the business environment over others in order to separate the important from the trivial

3. *Skill.* Demonstrates mastery or virtuosity over the financial and nonfinancial aspects of business— possesses a foundation for understanding people, organizations, and the way work is accomplished

4. *Form.* Combines myriad communications, structures, policies, etc., into a unified, coherent whole

5. *Representation.* Produces nonobvious and captivating ways of conveying meanings as opposed to giving simple directives and making straightforward declarations of fact

6. *Imagination.* Makes surprising and unconventional departures from the ordinary that create a new sense of awareness or understanding

7. *Authenticity.* Presents stylistic distinctiveness that is an honest expression of individuality and personal beliefs

8. *Engagement.* Offers complex and challenging information that encourages intellectual effort and imaginative contemplation

9. *Pleasure.* Provides emotionally rewarding experiences that are shared among members of a group, promoting stronger interpersonal bonds and fostering personal growth and fulfillment

10. *Human significance.* Facilitates personal reflection about who one is, what is most important, what is culturally valuable, and what is possible

11. *Context.* Takes actions that are commensurate with institutional practices, customs, demands, and norms, adopting a style of communicating that is understandable and appropriate under given circumstances

12. *Criticism.* Is an assessment of the leader's behaviors, where the effects of those behaviors invite critical discourse and evaluation from others regarding how well a person performed and the amount of appreciation he or she should be afforded

Satisfying all these criteria is difficult, and it is possible to recognize leadership archetypes when certain criteria stand out to the exclusion of others. For example, there are the humanistic types who never miss a birthday, who sponsor team dinners at the house, who go out of their way to accommodate employees, and who try to make the workplace pleasurable, enriching, and fun. There are the traditionalists who only do what is prescribed by "the book" and would never contemplate deviating from what a businessperson is supposed to wear, say, or do. There are the skillful technicians and bureaucrats who manage numbers and sheets of paper and who attempt to orchestrate every conceivable employee behavior through carefully planned and rigid sets of rules, compensation designs, policies, and organizational structures. There are the wildly imaginative but nondeclarative shape-shifters who hop from one idea and initiative to the next, dragging befuddled employees along in their wake. We could go on, but you see how this exercise works, and you can readily identify leaders you have known in which some aspects of our criteria are prominent and others are depressed.

One item notably missing from our list is character. We didn't consider it a stand-alone criterion, but it does figure into our discussion of criticism. Specifically, a leader or artist's personality, mannerisms, and beliefs may affect how receptive others are to the person's messages and consequent critiques—in extreme cases discounting the person's work entirely because viewers are unable to see through the person to the works he or she has produced. Regardless of how effective a person may be technically as a leader, it may be hard to appreciate that skillfulness if, for example, the person has unbecoming traits—perhaps he or she is slovenly, slightly twisted, unjust, or annoyingly intrusive. If every time you look at "X" you think of "Y," then whatever X has to offer will be muted or disqualified because of interference from Y.

Character clearly is important to leadership, and we have described basic traits that are critical to a leader's success elsewhere. These are compassion, gratitude, humility, humor, integrity, and sincerity.[2] Collectively, these attributes make great leadership possible, or, in their absence, difficult. Their presence does not assure leadership excellence, but it does set the range of potential. This means that some people will never excel at leadership because their character will never permit them to develop fully or to execute with nuance and craft. For example, the traits we name above will affect a person's ability to accept feedback from others and to acknowledge employees' efforts. These, respectively, are crucial to learning and to spurring motivation—both essential to leadership development and execution. It helps to have characterological advantages. We have met many people who simply are incapable of leadership above a threshold of "adequate," and some leaders who have no business whatsoever having authority over others because they are too compromised. We appreciate that in an egalitarian society where anyone is supposed to be able to achieve anything, this conclusion may be unsatisfactory and difficult to accept. Nevertheless, not everyone can be a great artist, and not everyone can be a great leader. We will have more to say about the characterological aspects of leadership in Chapter 12.

You may have noticed that one other criterion is not on our list: results. Shouldn't a good leader get results? The answer to that cliffhanger lies in Chapter 13. We can only answer that question in the context of the criteria that we are yet to discuss in detail. We can telegraph our outlook by saying that results often unduly diminish our interest in and our perceived need for leadership, but the issue of how financial and nonfinancial outcomes fit into the bigger picture certainly is a significant one and must await its due treatment until later.

All the ensuing chapters, except the final three, are organized in the same way. Each chapter addresses one criterion. The chapter begins with a question that you should ask yourself. The question reflects one of the principal meanings of the criterion, and if you don't have an answer in mind, we hope the information within the chapter will help you to find one.

After the question, we provide a short art-related vignette that highlights a point or two we subsequently will discuss. Even if you are not a connoisseur of the arts, we think you will appreciate the illustration as a way to highlight ideas in vivid, memorable ways. We have tried to represent most of the arts as examples for the sake of diversity and as a wide-ranging attempt to appeal to the varied interests of readers. Most important, however, we sample from the range of arts because certain arts exemplify a given criterion more effectively than others. Obviously, given the abundance of art, we had to narrow our choices from millions of works to 12; we are certain that other, better illustrations exist, but we have done our best to use accessible cases.

Following that, we explore the criterion in more depth, examining what it is, why it is important, and how it applies in business. We have purposely kept the book short, and therefore we do not offer an exhaustive list of applications in the text. Nevertheless, as an additional aid, we have supplemented the material on each criterion with a case study in the final chapter. Specifically, we apply our criteria to a mythologized executive to showcase how an evaluation might be conducted using the processes and criteria described in this book. We rely on secondary materials from several sources and personal experiences to formulate the core of our composition, fitting in miscellaneous information as needed to fill out the description. Therefore, the example should be interpreted as illustrative as opposed to an accurate portrayal of an actual person.

C. S. Lewis once remarked that philosophy is the study of what we already know. We would put leadership in the same camp. A common lament from those who read leadership books is that it is all common sense. What else could it be? Leadership is about a relationship between one person and others. As a relationship, it is subject to the same human interests and concerns that infiltrate other areas of our lives. Therefore, if we are accused of common sense, to that we would say, "Good, it should be." Both leadership and art are intimately connected with our daily affairs and to living a good life.

Nevertheless, common sense can be delivered in different ways. By asking you to think of yourself as an artist and of leadership as your art, we hope we will have given you novel means to consider your enterprise: a new script, as it were, for common sense that may prove especially helpful to you in the office or on the factory floor. There is one thing more to say that isn't so common, and we would be remiss in letting it slip by in our introductory remarks: people depend on you. When they look to you as a leader, they are asking more of you than what is implied by your job title, no matter how ornamental that title may sound. They must live with the successes or failures of your work. It matters a great deal how well you do it. If you call yourself a leader, you are inviting a special look from others who will study the evidence and make a conclusion about whether the label should be forfeited or duly honored. There is no escaping the profound responsibility that comes with leadership or the expectations of those who are counting on you to practice your art well.

# Chapter 1

# Intent: Leadership Begins in the Mind

## Question: What am I trying to accomplish?

*Impression—Sunrise*, Claude Monet
(Photograph: Getty Images)

Claude Monet was familiar with the new research on perception and light in the second half of the nineteenth century, including the work of French chemist Michel Chevreul (Chevreul originally worked with carpet dyes and later wrote a treatise on the way we see colors and, in particular, on the optical effects of neighboring colors). Monet's fascination with visual perception prompted a lifelong ambition to "paint the air": to study and represent how light breaks up on and between objects and how it scatters on reflective surfaces such as water. In one phase of his work, Monet was concerned with the changing conditions in the atmosphere between objects—in the air—or what he referred to as the *enveloppe*. His *intent* was to capture the fleeting conditions that surrounded and encapsulated objects— the subtle poetry of rural light mainly found on his Giverny estate and in neighboring fields. Specifically, he wanted to depict how weather conditions, seasonality, and the time of day influenced how we perceive objects.

In producing the atmospheric effects, Monet experimented with different ways in which people perceive—how they complete images with their minds. He understood that what he painted need not strictly correspond to actual spatial relationships and physical properties found in nature. An early example of his exploration into color and light can be seen in his historically important *Impression—Sunrise*. The atmosphere is everywhere as a blend of continuous hues, and Monet used indefinite boundaries to create the impression of a shimmering, pulsating sun. Interestingly, the sun stands out even though its actual brightness (luminance) is indistinguishable from the surrounding clouds.

Later, when Monet began his series on the Rouen Cathedral, his focus was again on atmospheric conditions and light. Visually, he wanted to understand the dynamic interplay of light with its subject, in this case, the French Gothic stonework exterior. At dawn, he bathed the arched portals, windows, and spires in cool tones of blue, pale pink, and purple. At sunset, he saturated the façade with fiery oranges and gold. The results stunned his audience. He analyzed London's Parliament, Venetian architecture, haystacks, poplars, and lily ponds with the same passion and intent. All are well-known subjects in his groundbreaking series of paintings. A technical perspective informed his work, but he didn't limit his understanding to current scientific color theory and advances in photography. He also embraced a global perspective through the study of Japanese woodblock prints. Acknowledging Hiroshige and other Japanese masters, he applied new compositional and design elements to his own works. Monet imagined the intangible and made it palpable through thick brushstrokes and dabs of electrifying color. At the same time, he made tangible structures seemingly dissolve, liquefy, or disintegrate on his canvas through a fusion of shimmering, atmospheric charge. The result of his extraordinary grasp of color and light was impressionism, one of the most dazzling and innovative movements in art history.

---

## ACTION AND ACCOUNTABILITY THROUGH INTENT

The most arresting lesson from Monet is that the life of wonderful works begins as an abstraction—as a vague concept that the artist is invested in refining and realizing. As with art, leadership too is the embodiment of an idea. We usually refer to these ideas as *vision*; however, we think that word is overused and feeds the egotism of leaders. We prefer to use the word *intent* because it is naturally coupled with behavior, whereas vision is not. Too often the production of vision statements is a stand-alone exercise with no forward thrust: meaningful strings of words with no impetus behind them. On the other hand, intent is the immediate precursor to action. Intentions keep us focused on what is most important to us and guide our behaviors accordingly. In addition, unlike vision, intent situates responsibility. When the author of an idea states what he or she is trying to do, there is no question who is supposed to do it.

Intent, perhaps, finds its nearest expression in a company's mission statement, but again, we think intent has advantages for its:

1. Intuitive, compact simplicity

2. Clarity and specificity—as opposed to nebulous wishful thinking

3. Usability throughout the organizational hierarchy

4. Unambiguous link to action and accountability

Indeed, vision and mission have become the products of ritualistic corporate exercises that rest inertly on walls or in corporate promotional materials as camouflage for the real business of making money. If the mission were so important, then presumably you would know what yours is. Do you? Intentions cut through corporate-speak by which we exhaustively dissemble vision, mission, objectives, and goals, often getting trapped in the minutiae of an esoteric exercise and losing sight of our true aims. All we really want to know is, "What is the problem you are trying to solve, and what are you going to do about it?" The specific aims generally are to enhance the organization's ability to compete by improving upon the many facets of innovation, operational efficiency, and executional excellence. At the highest corporate levels, expressed purposes may include bringing families closer together, promoting healthier lifestyles, making people happier, and nourishing the human spirit. Like Monet's strivings, these intentions are fantastic, and their resolution can only be loosely planned. The problems are difficult, poorly defined, and open to many possible solutions, some of which only will become apparent over time. If you want to achieve the impossible, then you will have to be able to live with ambiguity, periodic setbacks and disappointments, and occasional self-doubt.

## Lifelong Path to Excellence

You should prepare yourself for a lengthy and trying exercise. One of the most notable aspects of Monet's work is that he devoted himself to his self-imposed problem for decades. He was consumed by getting it right. While he could have been resting peaceably on his estate in his later years, he continued his rigorous exploration of light and color. Once started, a journey of this magnitude is never entirely satisfactorily concluded. There is always more to do and to perfect. On the other hand, had Monet's intentions initially been fame and fortune, there would have been a logical end state. In that case, there is nothing special to work on except how to mingle with the right crowd and accumulate wealth. The effort shifts from making real art to producing agreeable re-creations and cultivating public relations. Similarly, if your purposes are to acquire power, enrich yourself, and control a vast corporate empire, the skills you will need for success will be quite different than if your ultimate aims are sublime. The great artists of the Salon or workplace have more enduring and uplifting motives and intentions than vainglorious ones.

The best leaders we have watched and spoken with over the years all have one thing in common: early in their careers, they all wanted to excel at their craft, which included managing others well. Therefore, they commenced a lifelong study into the nature of leadership and, from their formative years onward, carefully observed how others succeeded and failed at it. They were able to learn from others because they were looking at the right things, importing into their behavioral repertoires what they believed they could use someday. They borrowed from the best, seeking out their feedback and advice and gradually fashioning an image of an ideal of their own. When someone tries, something magnificent happens: even the clumsiest improve. People really do get better if they have in their minds the kind of workplaces they want and the types of leaders they wish to be. If what they eventually hope to achieve conflicts with a company's brand of leadership and associated culture, they pack up and go where they can express themselves. These exits aren't atypical. Many of the more entrepreneurial and talented leaders leave and start their own companies because they know that their version of leadership will never be realized where they are.

## Intentions Are for Everybody

Anyone at any level of the organization who has responsibility for others can think big, *relative to the position*. A misconception has proliferated that leaders are only those who sit at or near the top of an organization and that the term *leadership* is reserved for them alone and misapplied to everyone else. Those accountable for others below the executive ranks are conceived as managers—simple craftspeople carrying out orders from above, according to a prescribed plan. In truth, leadership is exhibited throughout the organization, with the caveat that what a person hopes to achieve typically will be less grand at lower levels of the organization. The defining characteristic of leadership is not the number of people to whom it applies: the total staff that are supervised and one's position within the corporate pyramid. Therefore, unlike others, we consider differences between managers and leaders a matter of degree, not of kind. Monet was able to think lofty thoughts and have colossal ambitions because he knew he could. Monet had an established trail of careful study, practice, trial and error, and successes. He knew the extraordinary was within his reach. Thus, *intentions are hemmed in by true ability*. Intentions, then, have a close connection to talent and experience, but a person isn't disqualified as an artist or a leader simply because of inexperience. The neophyte, like everyone else, can imagine and try until others begin to notice—or realize he or she should take up another occupation.

## Intentions Are Made in Context

It is clear that Monet understood one other thing in his works: the abilities of his audience. He knew he didn't have to paint reality as we literally see it in order for his works to be perceived and understood in the way he wanted. He counted on the sensibilities of his audience, and he understood what those sensibilities were. Intentions, then, are related to the anticipated reactions of employees, customers, distributors, and such. Intentions incorporate others. As it happens, some artists and leaders may reach too far and find an audience that is unprepared for, or unable to hear, that which is communicated. This doesn't mean you shouldn't stretch the powers of your audience: it just means you may not be immediately rewarded for your efforts. In fact, *Impression—Sunrise* was not initially well received, nor was Monet in his stylistically formative years initially embraced as part of the inner circle: as a Salon exhibitor. Nevertheless, it makes no sense to reflexively accuse employees of being a bunch of thankless philistines who did not understand what you were attempting to say. A part of the leader's job is to gauge people's aptitudes. We are reminded of an admonition attributed to Franklin Roosevelt that "a good leader can't get too far ahead of his followers." For example, leaders who want to make their companies the most socially responsible would not have had the same reception for that idea in 1980 as they do today.

## Avoiding the Mean of Mediocrity

Three things get in the way of bold intent. The first is failing to believe in yourself and what you are able to accomplish. You can hold yourself back from trying because of psychological factors that may be summed up, behaviorally, as a lack of confidence. Second, you may be surrounded by unenlightened managers who impose their own lack of imagination onto others. You may, therefore, find yourself fighting the forces of mediocrity. Finally, you may have some really bad ideas. The reason many people would be precluded as leaders is because they are unable to articulate what they are trying to do. Or when they do conceive and announce their ambitions, their aims are commonplace—it's what all the other people in business say they are trying to do as well. How many times do we need to hear about cost cuts, shareholder value, or improved margins as breakthrough ideas?

## Ideas Within Your Grasp

Remedies exist for all these obstacles. Briefly, a corporate culture that encourages risk taking and accepts intelligent mistakes may alleviate the fear of trying. If you want more daring leaders, then a company needs to make *some* allowance for human error. As for uninspiring managers, first and foremost, you cannot allow their shortcomings to be your excuse for inaction. You need to figure out a way past them, and to be sure to get the credit you deserve should you succeed (bad managers have a knack for taking undue credit and transferring blame). If the situation appears futile, then the best alternative may be to look for more hospitable ground elsewhere. Finally, if you are having a hard time thinking up the equivalent to the impossible, you have a variety of options: brainstorm and test ideas with colleagues, get a coach who can help you to think through possibilities, or simply push yourself to think outside the confines of everyday duties, the standard job description, and the conventional outcomes they entail. This is your chance to transform a workplace that for far too many has become an uninspiring necessity.

## Appreciation Only of Purposeful Action

Intention is critical to leadership because it distinguishes serious attempts to lead from the mindless doodlings of dilettantes. We would be hard pressed to call a person's work "leadership" in the absence of any overarching challenge and goal. If a leader isn't trying to do anything particularly demanding, then what is it we are supposed to look at and evaluate? How are we to applaud what the leader has done? We only attach value to human actions when they are performed with purpose: the value lies in human creation. We appreciate the architect of a work when it is of his or her making as opposed to a consequence of happenstance. In summary, intention counts toward leadership because it represents the leader's commitment to realizing an idea. If a leader has no good ideas or lacks a desire to see reasonable ideas through to fruition, then that leader had better excel in some other way since he or she certainly will fail on this criterion.

# Chapter 2

# Focus: Emphasizing the Center of Attention

**Question: How will I focus, or frame, the action on what is most important without relying exclusively on words?**

From *Welcome to Nowhere (bullet hole road)*, Temporary Distortion
(*Welcome to Nowhere* by Temporary Distortion. Left to right: Lorraine
Mattox, Ben Beckley, and Brian Greer. Photograph: Jon Weiss.)

We could have used many theatrical images to illustrate the concept of focus, including the standard stage shot with spot lighting dripping on a sole actor, or perhaps an open-air amphitheater where the land gently slopes down and inward, converging on the focal point of the action. In either case, these rote depictions do not completely illustrate what live performances are and what their affiliated spaces do. Therefore, we elected to use a scene from a modern avant-garde play that toys with spatial relations as a way to reinvigorate an old truth: live productions are social constructions that have a lengthy history.

In fact, the original meaning of a stage—and we are going back a few thousand years—denoted any covered place, including theaters, tents, and temples.[1] These places served two functions. First, they were spaces that demarcated the everyday, ho-hum world from the world inside. Second, since we don't frame just anything, the space inside promised members, visitors, and audiences an invigorating and powerful experience, whether it was used to honor the gods, observe wedding vows, or stage a cathartic tragedy.

Creating something alluring doesn't occur by accident. Once a place has been framed by its physical attributes, and the expectant audience is positioned within the observational space, something has to happen. In addition, that something has to be different from what is routinely available in our daily lives. We attend the theater in anticipation of new, arresting experiences. The structural frame for action, whether a facility simply dressed with banners and flags or ornately decked out with precious metals, statuary, and rare paintings, elevates the excitement. A host of other aids, notably referred to as *mise en scene* ("putting on stage"), contributes to the total experience by directing onlookers' attention to the production through nonverbal means: the set, the positioning and movements of the actors, the music, the costumes, the props, the lighting, and so forth. They are all used in combination to create a distinctive and memorable world that enlivens the content of the action and intensifies our experiences. Therefore, the transformation of the ordinary is often facilitated through nonnarrative means.

All theater directs the audience's gaze, but theatergoers today typically discover that the play is the script, and we follow the words and base our interpretations on what is said. Much theater is literary theater, and the center of gravity is what is spoken. The avant-garde stage movement, and the reason for our illustrative selection, is because it demonstrates just how much punch live performances can have with original staging and limited actor interactions and exchanges. The illustration we have used from the theater group, Temporary Distortion, makes the point in the extreme. This ensemble has a reputation for staging unsettling, meditative performances in claustrophobic, box-like structures that feature minimal physical movements in which the performers never make eye contact, never touch, and barely move. Despite these self-imposed constraints, their plays are able to stirringly hit their marks through the use of beautiful video images, subtle gestures, original acoustics and music, and carefully selected cues.

The frames on paintings act in the same manner as frames around action in live performances. They isolate the work from their surroundings and accent meanings. Reframe a work, and the meaning changes with it. Vermeer's *Girl Asleep* would not have the same effect without the use of a frame that provides the sensation that we are looking in on a private space. Many artists including Whistler, Degas, and Seurat were adamant about the design and inclusion of frames on their works: Seurat was known to paint dots (in his pointillist technique) on his frames to underscore the fact that the frame was to be considered a part of the work.[2]

We often try to steer, order, and arouse through talk, talk, talk. But words aren't enough. They have their inspirational moments, and yet words alone make sorely incomplete and short-lived dramas. It is up to the entire ensemble of artists to help us to see what they want us to see by directing and sustaining our attention in innumerable ways so as to expand our sensibilities and awareness, and to enable more fascinating and deeply felt experiences. They do this by making choices about how they will create an aesthetic identity for their work.

---

## Producing a Framework

The best way to handle the leadership parallels to art in this chapter is by means of an imaginative exercise in which we ask you to think about going to a play that just arrived in your town and that you have wanted to see for a long time. The thought experiment is to reflect on the timeline from the day you ordered your tickets for the show through its completion. Here are a few things we believe you will experience, and we ask that you bear with us as we move back and forth between leadership and art. We believe that the parallels will be evident.

### The Company's Allure

It usually is the case that the best plays are the hardest to get in to because more people want tickets. You feel pretty good if you are fortunate enough to be one of the lucky few. The same holds in business. A part of the excitement is getting in to a place you perceive as highly desirable. In this regard, plays and business have two things in common. First, there is substantial self-selection. The people who want in are those who are attracted to what the ostensive offering is and are not just hunting for a seat or a job. Well, that's the way it should be. Companies that offer something of value will lure people who are looking for more than just something to do for a few hours each day, as a playgoer is looking for more than a place to sit—besides, there are more comfortable seats elsewhere. Second, there is a screening process that determines who will be included or excluded from entry, and it works two ways. Although an employee may meet the selection criteria and want to join for the right reasons, it is possible he or she will decline the offer because the company hasn't provided the precise job he or she wanted (seating is too far up and away from the stage), or it can't meet logistical concerns (for example, being unable to accommodate family-related matters). On the other hand, in business, people may be turned down because they don't fit the profile of someone who will succeed (they aren't going to enjoy the show) and will spend their time fidgeting until they reluctantly wait for the end or sneak out at intermission. The point is that focus begins well in advance of formally becoming an employee through the promotion of what a company uniquely has to offer and the selection process that explores mutual interests and fit.

## Anticipatory Excitement

We have spent enough time on trains into New York on matinee days for Broadway shows to have noticed the barely restrained excitement of those, finely dressed, heading for the theater. It is a very revealing contrast to the businesspeople who are far less eager and, most often, half asleep. The anticipation often is enhanced by a preparatory hook such as an advertisement that plants an idea that is difficult to get out of one's head about the future encounter. For a musical, it can be a song that one is familiar with and enjoys singing in the shower—the thought of seeing it performed live by a professional on stage, fully clothed, is a scintillating expectation. A business cannot produce the same anticipatory pleasures every day, but there should occasionally be hints that something exciting will take place. This could be news of the start of a fresh, promising project, the development and introduction of a new product, the prospect of international travel and exposure to a new line of business, or awareness of a forthcoming assignment in which one will use abilities that are rewarding to exercise. There are only so many times you can make the same trip to the same playhouse before the thrill wears off, unless the artistic director changes the show every now and then.

Those who are eager to get to their destination, theatergoers and businessgoers alike, have something they believe is a worthwhile place at which to arrive. But new employee or old, premier businesses, including arts organizations, actively regulate the anticipatory process and reinforce the excitement once people are on the premises. One easy way to achieve this end is by knowing that people are on their way and caring once they are there. We can recount many horror stories of employees' first days in which no one knew of the employee's arrival or even knew the person's name ("I'm sorry, who are you again?"). Unfortunately, this example always seems to remain current. Just when we think it is trite and are reluctant to use it, someone regales us with a recent misadventure. It is a telling experience that employees should seriously take note of.

Good organizations think their employees are special and are pleased that they have elected to join the company. They can demonstrate this delight on an ongoing basis through simple gestures such as creating attractive employee-only entranceways (not passageways used for deliveries), making accommodations for basic personal needs such as a place to stow a purse or nurse a baby, and taking the time for occasional remembrances such as birthdays and anniversaries pegged to hiring dates. Such forms of concern also imply that someone is attentive to a person's ability to enjoy the show or, in the case of business, be productive. Is the person comfortable? Are the surroundings conducive to enterprise? Does the individual have the tools needed to perform? Does he or she require any special accommodations in order to continue to perform well?

Some companies we have encountered have morning or periodic rituals where they pay respect to groups that otherwise get little attention and feel neglected. These may be the people who, out of sight from the core office dwellers, go out on the road every day to fix equipment; the back-office workers who silently copy, deliver, scan, stock, and file; or others such as the maintenance crew who are relegated to working under fluorescent lighting in the "garden level" of the office complex. The theater only differentiates with seating arrangements, but otherwise both businesses and playhouses are thankful that everyone is there and, most notably, will come back. The theater wants lifelong patronage as much as companies and employees want generative lifelong employment. To achieve that, everyone must feel welcome. It takes some guts to deviate from strict business protocols, but we once advocated formal ceremonies where truck mechanics periodically were given tools to recognize their service and expertise, and we recommended a book parade for book stackers who worked in cavernous conditions to thank them for their unseen contributions to a major institutional library. Offbeat? Yes. Effective? Yes. Fun? Yes.

## Setting Daily Expectations

Some companies start the day with the equivalent of handing out theater programs, letting employees know what they can expect, who will be involved, what is the anticipated resolution—holding informative team meetings so that everyone knows what needs to be accomplished that day in the service of more distal goals.

But most companies want people to just get busy. If everyone is engaged in simple repetitive tasks, then getting busy is easy enough, but that sort of work environment is unlikely to excite or produce anything out of the ordinary. Thus, "setting the stage" is critical in shaping people's daily outlook and is essential in preparing them for what is important and what is not, what to spend time on and what to forgo. The idea is to spend a little time creating focused activities. Measure twice, cut once, and save time in the long run.

## Framing the Action

One definition of both art and leadership is "the distillation of chaos." It is an ability to choose the essential for presentation and eliminate the distractions. This is the central concept of this chapter and the reason we chose the illustration we did. The ultimate action of a company has to carefully and narrowly engage employees' attention in order to obtain results. This is tough to accomplish since words alone won't sustain focus. This is where a leader could use some original thinking. In the theater, there are conventions for illuminating spaces and directing attention through props, motion, stage setting, and so forth. How can you achieve the same effects in an organization? Each organization will answer this question differently and will adopt a unique way to define the contours of its action. To us, however, the question of focus extends well beyond the customary verbal articulations. The broader issue pertains to the best ways to maintain focus on a regular basis and keep the action tightly packed around behaviors of central concern. The conundrum of focus is how to regulate concerted attention without always having to tell people expressly what they should think or how they should be spending their time. The constant repetition infantilizes and irritates adults, who soon become habituated to the sole use of verbal messages. Besides, absent other signs, the progenitors of recycled words and slogans often mistake their articulations as embodiments for real progress.

We would instead recommend more elaborate staging in each leader's respective area that avails itself of all senses to make a recurring point of where employees should concentrate their efforts. We can't say that we have seen companies produce a focused show very frequently, but theatrical devices are at your disposal. For example, we are presently working with the mortgage service center of a bank. The center's primary job is to keep people from being foreclosed upon, i.e., keep people in their homes. The company could film the gratitude customers feel when their home is preserved and their lives are literally saved. It could have a light flash on when a loan is successfully restructured. Or as we once did within a call center, the company could select a call of the week in which an employee did an exceptional job and sit in the round and listen to and, subsequently, discuss the conversation. The employee gets well-earned attention, and others present get the point. If you use your imagination, another criterion we address later, then you can maintain a much sharper focus at work. The main obstacle is fear of what others who are less "businesslike" will think.

## Maintaining Focus

Quite a few distractions can interfere with corporate focus. Not everything goes as planned, and it is easy to perseverate on all the things that have gone wrong instead of on what the workforce could be doing right to move ahead. Leaders can easily lose the focus of their teams if they allow past failures to dominate their mental states. We believe it was Michael Jordan who placed a self-imposed one-hour time limit to reflect on a game before once again turning his attention toward the future. Katherine Hays, a former rower and now chief executive of the visual effects company GenArts, makes the point that leaders can't be distracted by the fact that they may be a little behind. Or, conversely, teams can't spend too much time congratulating themselves for something well done. The idea of both Jordan and Hays is that if you want to be successful over the long haul, you can certainly notice where you are and how things are going, but you also must quickly put the past behind you in order to immerse your team once again in what it can do better and what it has to do next.[3]

# Skill: If You Are Incapable of Doing It, It Can't Be Done

**Question: Do I have full command of the medium, methods, and techniques that will allow me to excel?**

*The Burghers of Calais*, Auguste Rodin
(Photograph: Getty Images)

The *Burghers of Calais* by Auguste Rodin was a monument commissioned by the civic leaders of Calais in 1884 to commemorate the heroism of six men who saved the town during the Hundred Years' War. Through a slightly convoluted bit of reasoning involving intermarriages and ancestral claims, Edward III conceived of France as southern England and invaded it. When the town of Calais was conquered, six burghers volunteered to sacrifice their lives in exchange for the safety of the townspeople. The king agreed and requested the burghers come to him plainly clothed (shirts and breeches) and barefooted, with nooses around their necks.

We will resume the story momentarily, but first, in keeping with the chapter's topic, we will discuss Rodin's preparation for this magnificent work. As you might imagine, Rodin could not have created this sculpture unless he had mastered the medium in which he worked. The artistic media are the materials used to influence the perceptions of viewers. The materials, across the arts, are the oils, bronze, movements, meter, wood, canvas, notes, rhythm, pitch, shape, and so on. If artists do not perfect their techniques and understand the capabilities and limitations of their materials, greatness will elude them forever. The materials must be expertly manipulated to obtain the expressive potential of the work.

Rodin's training was long and difficult. While he attended a school for the decorative arts as a youth, as a young man, he was repeatedly refused admission into the prestigious École des Beaux-Arts. Instead, he served a lengthy apprenticeship under the successful and productive sculptor Albert-Ernest Carrier-Belleuse. Rodin also traveled to the artistic havens of Europe, examining the various styles employed during different historical periods. His patience and education eventually paid off when his first work was accepted by the Salon in Paris. This did not occur until he was 37 years old, and even then, his piece was poorly received.

Over time, he acquired an unrivaled gift for modeling plaster and clay. He could adeptly sketch figures as well. The ability to produce a sculpted model in plaster, clay, stone, or marble is, of course, the foundation of a work. Yet to produce a bronze of the quality of the *Burghers*, Rodin also had to understand the delicate wax casting process he used to convert the model into bronze: delicate because it is imperative to convert a clay model into a bronze sculpture without losing the original details. In addition, unlike many sculptors of the period, Rodin spent a great deal of time finishing the bronze cast by chasing (creating indentations to produce lighting effects), applying chemical treatments to alter the patina, or coloring, of the bronze, and hand-polishing with a chamois. To achieve the effects he wanted, Rodin had to know where to make indentations, apply acids, and such. The idea of surface treatments was later adopted by other sculptors such as Giacometti and Brancusi.

There is one other aspect to the use of the medium which, as promised, takes us back to Calais. The city leaders were not pleased by Rodin's work. First, the anguished souls lacked nobility: in fact, they looked like ... people, and not well dressed ones at that. It was customary to use professional models for sculptures, but Rodin tended to use ordinary street people instead. Second, Rodin violated convention in at least three other ways. Most monuments were mounted on pedestals, but Rodin wanted the sculpture placed on stepping-stones: at the same level as the observer. It also was standard practice to have some order to multiple figures, but the burghers seem confused and in disarray—they are, after all, off to be killed. Third, usually, one person stands out above others in a classical pyramid shape (this would have been the first burgher to volunteer his life), but Rodin treated them equally. He also used the same parts more than once (to unify the work and produce a sense of dynamism) and gave the burghers extra-large hands and feet (as if anchored by the weightiness of their decision). In order to fully exploit the medium, then, and promote full appreciation of the work, there is another skill to master: how and where to position and present the work.

Taken together, it is impossible to look at great art without simultaneously appreciating the formal properties and technical skills required to create it, including those infinitely small but all-important decisions regarding arrangement. As we hope we have shown, there are many layers of skill required to produce what Rodin accomplished, and still stands, in Calais.

## PRACTICE, PRACTICE, PRACTICE

Whatever Rodin's natural gifts may have been, he honed them over a very lengthy period of study. He did not miraculously become a great sculptor. In fact, we can't think of any individuals offhand who accomplished anything of significance without first dedicating themselves to a discipline and preparing for the inevitability of lifelong learning. The latter point is worthy of emphasis: because art changes, the artist has to change along with it. The same applies to leadership. It is not something that is learned. It is something one learns and continues to learn indefinitely. Leaders who understand that they are engaged in an occupation that requires study are ones who find mentors, learn from their own mistakes, test new methods, speak to others about their approaches, take classes, read books, and improve over the years as a result.

There are elementary skills to be perfected if one is to have any chance at success at leading others. We would say that it starts with a love of the constituent materials and an appreciation for what they are capable of producing. In leadership, that means people. It is possible to get a batch of bad clay; and people, too, may disappoint. But at heart, if leaders don't have affection for the people who depend upon them, we do not see how they can ever excel. Great leaders don't curse the resourceful variability of people. Rather, they embrace the infinite possibilities, the nuances, the personalities, and, at times, the miraculous. A predicate of leadership achievement is a foundational love of people and their individual aspirations.

## Technique

In addition to having a genuine appreciation for and understanding of people, no leader can be great without being technically competent. In fact, we would have to say that a good many leaders we have seen had no credibility with staff because they lacked the requisite knowledge of their discipline and had poorly developed business acumen. We can't think of anything more frustrating to an employee than turning to a leader for advice and receiving nothing in return. If in response to "How do I do this?" the recurring answer is "I don't know" or "Let me check on that and get back to you," it will be difficult to rebound as a qualified leader since employees will circumvent the leader in the future, going elsewhere for advice—struggling to work things out independently. These clueless leaders obtain their positions through favoritism or through bosses who lack proficiency and perpetuate incompetence; or in some cases they were hired at a time when their skill set was relevant, but they have since been left behind.

It is the leader's job to possess ample expertise so as to be of value to others. This doesn't imply the need to know the answer to every possible contingency that may arise, but to know enough to consider the relevant variables. It also is the leader's job to fully understand the context in which people work. That includes knowing the fundamentals of the industry and related industries, the business content and imperatives of the specific discipline, the operating procedures and processes to efficiently accomplish the work, and the capabilities of people in order to use them to their fullest potential through proper placement.

We would insert the caveat that just because a leader (or "master" of the arts) knows the answer to a question or can tell what he or she would do in a particular circumstance, that doesn't mean the leader should reveal *his or her* answer. A central part of learning is quizzing people on their ideas and what they know, so they, too, can think deeply about the issues and come to their own conclusions. If necessary, they can then be corrected and their thoughts channeled in a slightly different direction.

A fair amount of technique is teachable and, we think, valuable, as long as the learning doesn't produce canned and predictable responses. A manager can learn how to communicate more effectively, to negotiate in a manner that preserves long-term relationships, to provide meaningful feedback, to listen more thoroughly, and to think more creatively. These skills can make you more effective if applied correctly, but they by no means constitute leadership in the aggregate. A frequent misconception is that leadership is no more than a bundle of skills. If applied incorrectly, they can backfire as insincerity. Some training we have observed over the years produces sterile, counterproductive results for the insecure or inept, instructing them on how to conduct programmed conversations, i.e., not really listening, not really communicating—more like a parrot than a leader.

## Tensile Strength

Leaders have a sixth sense ... they don't see dead people ... but they know how far and how long they can push their organizations until the people and materials begin to quiver and cracks begin to form. As we have heard fine leaders say, they know when to let up on the gas before the outcomes of their work are compromised. Because they understand people and the nature of the work, leaders know just how far employees can go before they need a rest. This rest may consist of a temporary project, a brief sabbatical, a redeployment, or even, as we have seen, a midday cookout. The respite doesn't have to be fancy or long; it just needs to have rejuvenating qualities that enable people to continue on without breaking. Since people get paid, we often think that the exchange is a simple one in which the worker carries out his or her part of the bargain by showing up for work and doing what the job requires. Even robotics on the assembly line, however, need to be taken offline periodically for maintenance, and so we are surprised when managers assume that people are more durable. Proper preparation and care of basic fundamental substances are hallmarks of a fine sculptor. If a sculptor were as negligent with his or her materials as some managers are with their people, the sculpture would never obtain the form and permanence that the artist wants.

One of the aims of great leadership is to look at people over the long run to make sure that their productivity remains high over time—that their energy is not expended and that they are not considered disposable. With any natural material, it is essential to know individuals' pressure points, tolerances for various stresses, psychological fractures, physical endurance, and so forth.

## Details

The beauty of a Rodin sculpture takes place after the bronze cast is completed. What gives the sculpture its elegance is the handiwork that is performed on the nearly completed piece, but the details make all the difference in the world. We often think of details as dotting $i$'s or crossing $t$'s: they are thought of as ancillary to the finished product, adding little value beyond a master plan such as the corporate strategy. In addition, the metaphor of finishing off letters presumes that these final touches are prescribed by established rules. Neither the assumption that details are subordinate to the big work nor the belief that they are entirely governed by rule is true in art or leadership.

For Rodin, the finishing touches, the details, were the defining characteristics of his pieces—neither superfluous nor necessary evils. Michael Woodford, the former CEO of Olympus Corporation, would certainly agree when he says, "I've always believed that what makes a company special are the little things."[1] Having a reputation for being a bit obsessive, he fastidiously attended to details, especially regarding the tracking, reporting, and sales of products—which is perfectly sensible to us since often the parts of organizations responsible for these matters can be loosely structured and free spirited. Great artists, a membership that would include Rodin, make choices about the details that give works their unique qualities and the effects they want.

Many replicas of Rodin's works have been made from his casts—thus, the reason you see several *Thinkers* sitting around. But the one we would want would be the one created by Rodin's own hands, the one where he thought about where to apply acids, make a dent, or produce a sheen. For those who fail to see value in the specifics, it is advantageous to rethink what details really are. They are tedious still, but nonetheless they are the elements that can distinguish the ordinary from the absolute. To us, the concept of "best practices," which we have never favored, is what makes something common without consideration of what further work could make it your own and distinctive. What best practices can't provide are answers to those infinite decisions and small details that can transform the usual program or approach into an extraordinary one.

## Perspective and Communication

In assessing which details are important, one of the chief concerns is perspective: Who are the members of the audience, and what will help them to understand and use the program or information being offered? What will help them make sense of your aims and the current state of affairs?

We often do things from rote or historical precedence, but consider how much less grand Rodin's piece would have been had he ignored the context of the event and presented the sculpture the town elders wanted—from their point of view. The central aspect of the piece would have been lost if well-dressed and manicured clergy were elevated and aligned to face their deaths: the entire concept of sacrifice would have been diminished. The burghers' weightiness, their relative positioning, their disheveled appearance, and their humanity all reveal that real people prefer not to die. It is a sculpture as well as a monument, and perspective matters. Rodin could have propagated a great lie and created the piece the town patrons wanted: a work more concerned with appearances than reality. Or he could have created a lasting monument for future generations who could reflect on the courageous few who were willing to save the lives of many in sacrificing their own. Thankfully Rodin preferred to depict the burghers as they truly must have felt, capturing their point of view as doomed men. Rodin elected to conceive of the truth of the matter as he imagined it to be. And lo and behold, the statue still stands, commemorating the selfless gift the burghers gave to the city of Calais. Given the way the sculpture is portrayed, visitors today understand that meaning. The romanticized version of reality that the town leaders wanted would have been foreign to observers today, since even if the burghers deeply believed in life everlasting, they surely still would have had an investment in this world, too—the one where their feet met stones.

Leadership contains two underappreciated skills, both high-lighted in the Rodin piece. One is to recognize and communicate things as they are without the spin to which we have become all too accustomed. Leaders today think they are doing a good job when they are able to convince us, contrary to the facts, that everything is going according to plan. Without entering the political arena headlong (but think about America's long-term military presence abroad and the 10 years of reports of "significant progress"), we will merely say that there are plenty of contemporary examples to pull from. The other is the use of symbolism to reveal and underscore unspoken truths. Rodin weighed his figures down with disproportionate extremities: he gave them a dynamic, but it was slow and measured—the burghers weren't exactly rushing to their hanging. Rodin gave his work greater depth and substance by appending an affective component to the work so the processional could be fully appreciated for what it really was...a death march. In summary, leaders should assuredly display self-confidence and confidence in others, but one attribute they ought not to possess is covering the truth.

# Chapter 4

# Form: Putting It All Together

**Question: Have I assembled the various communicative devices into a coherent whole that presents a uniform message and direction?**

*Composition in Black and White, with Double Lines, 1934,* Piet Mondrian
(© 2012 Mondrian/Holtzman Trust c/o HCR International Washington, DC)

Form generally refers to the properties found within an artwork independently of other considerations from the work itself. In this regard, it is customary to speak about sensory experiences derived from the total composition or spatial organization of a piece, such as how lines, shapes, colors, textures, shininess, movements, sounds, and so on fit together to produce unity, or in the case of Piet Mondrian (originally Mondriaan—he dropped an *a* when he moved to Paris), harmony. Many of the artists of Mondrian's time, who stripped away content in order to put pure form on display, have periodically generated derogatives from the casual art-going public, "Even a child could do that." Unseen, however, is how artists like Kandinsky, Malevich, Klee, and Mondrian labored over their works and how their own art changed over time. In removing the figurative, these artists proved that there was a transcendent loveliness to basic forms that were capable of arousing emotion if assembled in the proper ways. The intricate interplay of basic elements could evoke aesthetic responses precisely because these forms touched a universal spiritual note.

Mondrian, indeed, was spiritual and was a student of theosophy, a blend of Eastern and Western religions. This may have been both a reaction to and a consequence of his strict Calvinist (Dutch Reformed Church) upbringing. Given his background and spiritual interests, it is, perhaps, a touch ironic that Mondrian wanted to demystify art by showing how much there is to be seen in the shapes that often are buried in our everyday world and that we otherwise fail to notice. In a sense, Mondrian was demonstrating in the visual arts what composers like John Cage were illustrating through musical pieces such as his 4' 33" (which if specified in seconds is 273, or absolute zero on the Celsius scale). The silent work of Cage shows how much we miss in the ambient sounds that surround us daily. If we were more attentive, we could hear these sounds more clearly and recognize that they have form, texture, and emotional valence.

Mondrian's art was the search for the absolute, and he thought he had found it in the rhythm, balance, and harmony of his work. He was a great space organizer and master tinkerer. As he listened to the jazz that he dearly loved, he would arrange and rearrange lines and shapes, thicken and narrow objects, and modify color positions until the work had the depth and significance he desired: an artist knows when a work is finished, when any further changes devalue the work in some fashion. He wasn't just slapping on paint; he carefully studied the relationships he created and moved objects around, refined colors and densities, and added luster, making deliberate self-conscious decisions to orchestrate the pictorial equivalent of jazz—a moving energetic force. He discovered that small things could carry great intensity and that small changes could redefine a work of art. A bit of nuance combined with artistic restraint could have dramatic effect, producing electrifying force and dynamism.

Importantly, for Mondrian, harmony does not imply symmetry or a center around which everything else relates and is organized. It is more complicated than that. Often, the most interesting aspects of his art take place around the edges. Harmony has more to do with elements that don't overpower one another, or with the equity of relationships. These elements are all manifest in this chapter's example, *Composition in Black and White, with Double Lines*, which recently sold at Sotheby's for $9.2 million. Although little is strictly symmetrical, the illusion of symmetry persists; there is a sense of balance and harmony even though the spacings between the lines are irregular, and the lines are of different densities and off center. Movement and dynamism are achieved by the bi-directionality of the lines, which forces viewers to explore the entire work before their gaze returns to its point of origin. In the end, you have before you the simple, transcendent work of a poet and romantic dreamer.

---

## PUTTING THE PIECES TOGETHER

The simple can be so beautiful. Although it isn't the main point we want to make in this chapter, it is the one that is most striking to us. Mondrian shows that carefully thought-out and effective compositions do not have to appear complicated. We would argue that the same is true in business. Each layer of complexity adds a new layer of inefficiency, error, and stodginess. People operate best when the lines are straight and clean. However, before you dictate that all processes be cleansed of excess, we must issue a warning first. It took Mondrian years to develop his style, and each piece he created was painstakingly crafted; he constantly reset his works until he was pleased with the results. But the process was long and arduous. Our warning, then, is this: minimal and uncomplicated is not the same as easy.

We recall many meetings with an executive group where there were debates about products, distribution, and all manner of business. People would spit out highly complex ideas regarding product enhancements, marketing ploys, and revised sales channels, mostly convoluted and impractical. The president, an older fellow, sat at the head of the table. He always looked like he was dozing off, head down, eyes closed, hands folded on a significant pouch of a belly. When people had finished parrying ideas, he would lift his head, smoothly synthesize the conversation to its bare essence, and ask if what they had in mind as a possible solution was "X." "Yes, that is exactly what we were trying to say," and they meant it. They weren't being sycophants, but had realized that their overly involved suggestions could be reduced to simpler, more cost-beneficial resolutions. The president had a way of astounding doubters who thought he was over the hill. He was over the hill in a way, but that's what enabled him to see the things on "the other side" that they couldn't. He had a rich knowledge of the terrain and was able to condense the complex into the simple because he had a deep understanding of the issues. Simplification is not something that occurs mystically: it requires a person like Mondrian or our friend who has given considerable thought to the issues, built a reservoir of expertise, and knows what he is doing. Finding simplicity is truly an art, and it is hard to do well.

## Finding the Hidden

One of Mondrian's gifts was an ability to visualize patterns through the clutter. In turn, he was able to expose forms to us that he considered to be of universal significance. He located value in what wasn't readily discernible. Most people become preoccupied with the visually handy, failing to consider what is absent or outside their perceptual field. In business, it always is prudent to ask, "What is missing from this picture?" It is easy to get misled by sticking only to what has immediate sensory import, forgetting that the unseen counts as evidence as well and may likely make the difference in what you decide to do.

We once worked with the sales function of a major pharmaceutical company whose executives insisted that the best salespeople were trained in the biological sciences and had experience in sales with other pharmacy companies (if they were not hired directly out of college). The correlation was evident, and the statement was accurate to a point: those people made good salespeople, just not the best. In the mass of data available, all the executives saw was what they already believed to be true. They missed the clear, replicable patterns beneath. There were better salespeople. We share Mondrian's vision of looking beyond the evident and searching out motifs that are less accessible but often of equal or superior value.

## Composition

The most revealing aspect of Mondrian's art lies in the composition: the way all the elements are represented and combined. Unity is one of those essential components of art that produces art's seductive effects. Unfortunately, there is no formula that defines unity. Otherwise, no artist would have to labor over decisions about the whats, hows, and wheres of design. You can think of arranging the top of your desk as an example of assembling elements into a whole. Some decisions are purely functional (e.g., you want to be able to get to your stapler easily), but others are purely aesthetic. There is no immediate purpose, and so the placement of your photos, clock, lamp, in-basket, etc., is dependent on what looks right to you based upon your prior experiences and distinct sensitivities. Organization, big or small, is mostly art with a few basic rules thrown in for good measure.

Whether we are concerned with art or business, the purpose of composition is the same. The overall product—either a discrete product such as an automobile or compound products such as entire organizations—must have relational content that conveys a consistent overall impression. (For example, contrast General Motors' hideously convoluted Pontiac Aztec of a decade ago with today's stylish, award-winning Cadillacs.) For Mondrian's works, composition meant the proper placement of lines and, for most of his works, primary colors. Summary impressions of businesses are conveyed through the organizational culture, which may be interpreted as the holistic meaning of its individual pieces. The same intensity and labor is involved in getting it right, as goes into a work of art. The last thing an artist would want to hear from an onlooker is, "I'm confused; I just don't get it; everything seems a jumble, and I get mixed messages; I don't know what he is trying to say." These would not be welcome words to a leader, either.

Yet, consider the enormity of the task. Let's suppose that the leader wants to communicate the desire for a service-centric organization. Nevertheless, the leader has a siloed organization with woefully splintered front-to-back-end service. He or she has a reward structure that excludes service as a performance measurement and includes incentives based on profits per customer. The organization has a weak and scattered selection process and makes no attempt to assess customer orientation for service-facing employees when hiring. There are no measures of customer satisfaction, or related indicators, taken. Those with direct contact with customers are evaluated on the speed of their handling times, and there is insufficient staff to provide adequate follow-up to problems. The company has decided that it is too expensive to take people offline for management and service training. Career progressions are entirely predicated on making money versus taking care of customers and playing nicely with others. The most prestigious department, telegraphed in different ways, is finance. Executives only visit with customers when there are major issues that could potentially be costly to the company; they don't seek out and speak with customers otherwise. Because of acquisitions and other factors, the information systems do not uniformly gather data at the customer level, and systems in different parts of the company fail to talk with one another—so what is known in one place about a customer is unknown elsewhere. By the way, we are describing a real company, one that we know you will recognize at least in the abstract. It is readily apparent that the desire for a service-centric culture in this company is a dream. It will remain so until the structure, the rewards, the systems, and the people are more harmoniously assembled. But that will require time, energy, and a true artist.

Organizations have to do many things simultaneously, and leaders always have to consider trade-offs and tinker with corporate arrangements. Perfect alignment of all organizational elements is impossible, although there will be abbreviated occasions when what you have done feels about right. Nevertheless, we prefer Mondrian's definition of harmony as a preferred way to think about what companies refer to as internal alignment: equity among elements. If you want a service-centric organization, don't allow organizational components to overpower the importance of service in the grand design. It won't be the only aspect of corporate success that matters, but keeping service from getting lost in the mix would be victory.

## Little Things That Make a Big Difference

The idea behind catastrophe theory is that little things can make a big difference. Despite what we learned in graduate school many years ago, the world isn't as linearly oriented as we once believed. Variables don't move neatly in step with one another. There comes a time when one step is a step too far. Mondrian noticed the same with the minuscule movements and densities of lines and colors. Small changes, big effect. The penchant of corporations for taking care of the "low-hanging fruit" has never been an approach we have championed. We have always favored first taking care of the little things that can kill you. The problem, of course, is that because the issues appear small at the time, few contingencies are planned around them. For example, a nominal cost reduction made to a product in the wrong places can have major effects on consumer behavior, contracting purchases that lead to another round of cuts and perpetuating a downward spiral until much of the quality has been removed from the product and buyers have ventured elsewhere. Our point is that quite often these adverse events happen gradually, with reductions in sales uniformly lagging the cost cuts until the product suddenly becomes something that customers will no longer buy, and revenues suddenly drop off the cliff like lemmings.

Toward the end of 2011, the U.S. Postal Service decided to eliminate one-day service to save money, offering instead two- to three-day expedited service.[1] We assume that the math behind the decision produced a positive result: the difference calculated was the cost savings against the lost one-day business to other carriers. We don't know what will happen over the longer term, but it is conceivable that this one change, along with the growing ease of use of new technologies, will lower organizational earnings for all types of deliveries by modifying consumer attitudes and habits and chasing consumers more quickly to electronic mail. We aren't just talking about unintended consequences. We are talking about a seemingly small change in operations within one entity that may have pronounced systemic effects across the entire industry. There is a potential net loss of customers throughout the paper delivery industry that will exponentially accelerate over time and, perhaps, not only for quick deliveries but for all deliveries for all carriers. Small ember, big burn.

# Chapter 5

# Representation:
# Many Ways to Say Things

**Question: Do I use a full range of methods of communication, including symbols, to unambiguously convey my points?**

*Sudden Shower over Shin-Ohashi Bridge and Atake,* Utagawa Hiroshige
(Brooklyn Museum, Gift of Anna Ferris, 30.1478.58)

The word *representation* often is used in verb form—to *represent*—like several other similar words: to *denote*, to *portray*, and so on. When using these words, we look for the object to which they refer. These are things, events, natural occurrences, theories, states of affairs, or concepts that a person wishes to convey, or communicate, to another. These referential objects are conveyed through the use of symbols that can be words, pictures, enactments, musical notes, or any other medium that can transcribe an idea into a message that is understood by others. The degree to which an artist is able to use representational content successfully in making his or her point is a measure of the artist's abilities. Representational success is generally measured by the impact it has on another: in general, better art elicits stronger emotional and ideational reactions.

The example in this chapter is a nineteenth-century woodblock by the artist Utagawa Hiroshige, and it is a counterexample of sorts. The illustration depicts a solitary boatman serenely poling his log raft downstream past the area known as Atake during a *yūdachi*—an evening descent of the thunder god responsible for the darkened sky and summer rain (the rice culture of the Japanese uses many different descriptors for different types of rain).[1] This print is the undisputed masterpiece of the series that later served as the inspiration for oils by Vincent van Gogh and James Whistler. Our temptation is to think of the poor people stuck crossing a bridge during a storm. But symbols always require a community of like-minded people, including the artist, who will depend on observers to make culturally relevant interpretations. It is easy to send the wrong message or have meanings understood in ways that were not intended when parties are operating from different assumptions, frames of reference, and cultural norms.

Rain is a popular theme in Japanese art and one rarely seen in Western art. Only a few Western artists have incorporated rain into their works, instead, preferring to portray rain in distant thunder clouds or as a dissipating shower accompanied by a sunny afterglow. That's because rain is bad in the West and good, or a positive force, in the East (We sing, "Rain, rain go away," while the Japanese children sing, "Rain, please rain"). Representation acts as a cultural bridge in the arts. Its purpose is, to draw on Shakespeare (*A Midsummer Night's Dream*, Act 5, Scene 1), to give "airy nothing a local habitation and a name"; in other words, to take an idea and imbue it with substance and meaning.

The artist's aim is to make stirring representations but, at the same time, to anticipate how the audience will see and react to the representation. There is plenty of room for misunderstanding, and it seems to us that the quality of the art and the clarity of the message are often inversely related. It takes more time and effort to interpret and assimilate more engaging art and less time to interpret the equivalent of tromp l'oeil, or mimetic reproductions—you get what you see and nothing more. In order to avoid erroneous interpretations, reduce the number of "that's not what I meants," and yet make a point in an extraordinary way, the artist must think about what the audience already knows: the works that have preceded this one; knowledge of the subject matter, customs, habits, and norms; something about the artist, including his or her intentions, life story, and style; and so on. In the end, what the artist is trying to communicate has to be visible to the intended audience.

One last thing complicates matters. In some arts, the artist doesn't control the ultimate message: intermediaries do, and different intermediaries will interpret messages in different ways unless explicitly told what to emphasize and de-emphasize. Even so, variations are still bound to occur. We are thinking of arts such as music, where it is up to the conductor and musicians to interpret a work, or theater, where interpretation depends on the director and actors. Interestingly, Hiroshige was known for allowing the visual equivalent of an intermediary by embracing brevity in his woodblocks. In addition to experimenting with scale (e.g., near and far, high and low: notice the boat in the background is as crisp as more proximal objects and appears elevated in the work), his works are uncluttered and empty. That is because he leaves it to us, the viewer, to fill in the details. The idea is to give us the space we need to complete the work based on our unique observations and experiences. He wants us to act like intermediaries who add value to the work through our own imaginations. The better the intermediary, the more interesting the work.

## Meaning Is Everywhere

A graph is a representation, e.g., of profits over time. The quarterly call with analysts is a representation, e.g., of the state of affairs of the company. The way you travel is a representation, e.g., of some aspects of your character. What can seem very straightforward, like rain, can be interpreted in myriad ways. We are surrounded by the symbolic, as it's our nature to find meaning in things. Much of what a leader does, then, is under microscopic scrutiny. Employees gather and collate their interpretations based on the aggregate of what they see. In the context of fine clothes, rare art, an oversized mansion, excessive compensation, a bevy of handlers, four wives (each younger than the last), and very little contact with the rank and file, a private plane may be interpreted as entitlement and lack of humility as opposed to an efficient mode of travel. Multiple messages are combined in a gestalt. The gestalt will evoke a set of expressive words such as *powerful, cunning, trustworthy, smart, compassionate, daring, unethical, gracious,* and the like. These naturally feed the degree to which a leader is admired or despised, which, in turn, influences interpretations of successive acts.

## Magnum Opus

Many artists have what may be their defining piece or group of pieces that most visibly puts their virtuosity on display and best represents what they were trying to accomplish. These are the works that elicit the most intense reactions in others and inspire the greatest sense of awe. These works frequently were the culmination of a personal challenge that can take various forms. The artist may want to prove that he or she could overcome the limitations of a certain material by, for example, giving the illusion of depth and color to a stone that does not naturally have those properties; or the artist may want to show the beauty of the human body in an astonishingly new way. Leaders, too, need their magnum opus: the set of representations that define them and their work. The recently retired Sam Palmisano of IBM may have sealed his legacy through his transformation of IBM into a high-margin services and analytics company. Through a cadre of representational acts including judicious acquisitions, he created a cultural bridge that traversed the gulf between a new idea and a new social reality. There is something to be said for leaders who have kept companies of IBM's size and scale rolling during a period of broad economic malaise. For good or bad, Palmisano has left something behind for which he will be known. Artists leave their imprimatur in their works, and we wait to see if time will be kind. For IBM, so far, so good.

## Multiple Audiences, Multiple Messages

In 1972, NASA launched the *Pioneer 10* spacecraft to explore the galaxy. In the event that this probe was seen by extraterrestrial life, we provided representations that expressed something about who we are. We inserted a plate into the craft that contained engravings of a naked man and woman, with the man's right hand raised as a gesture of fellowship and peace. In the unlikely case that *Pioneer* is reeled in by extraterrestrials, it is comical to think that alien creatures will have any clue of what we are trying to say, if anything at all. It is easy to envision aliens scratching their tentacles in confusion. Interpretation isn't a simple matter since not everything can be perfectly known. Even, for example, if an artist were to explain to us what he or she was trying to do, there would still be components of the work that would seem right but that the artist couldn't explain: room for interpretation abounds. That is, not even artists can tell us everything there is to know, and we need not accept their explanations if the facts seem contrary.

What we are left with are works that can be interpreted in different ways by different people. People have their own histories, interests, expertise, and perspectives, and that makes complete agreement on anything, from votes in city hall to the board room, very difficult. The possibility for misunderstanding requires the leader to anticipate how others will view and react to what he or she is representing. The leader, just like the artist, has to have a sensibility to the members of the audience and to their perceptual apparatus in order to be effective. The complicating factor, of course, is that the things a leader says and does are heard and seen by many. Rather than try to control the audience, then, we have always found it more fruitful to manage the interpretative range: to make sure that the representation succinctly articulates the intended message. Say what you mean; mean what you say.

It is easy to illustrate how leaders can confuse people. Josh Weston, the former CEO of ADP, is a friend of ours. He is a very nice guy, but ask all those who have ever worked for him what is unacceptable, and they will tell you that it is missing a deadline (with suitable diagnoses and results). That is because they always knew that the "call" was coming: "Where is it?" A leader can give an assignment which, as words only, represents his or her wishes for a particular outcome; but the more powerful associated representation is an irrefutable act that indicates the leader's interest in, and the perceived importance of, the results. One representation, the one with a request and no further action, remains open and subject to interpretation: the leader *may* want this, and the results *may* be important. With unerring follow-up, however, there is no dodging clarity and accountability; i.e., "When Josh asks for something, he really means it." The interpretative sphere has been tightened.

## Mediated Work

One of the interesting facets of art is that it frequently doesn't come straight to us from the artist. Film, theater, and symphonies all require a host of intermediaries to bring a work to life. Directors, actors, conductors, and musicians, for example, are called upon to deliver a message. These intermediaries put their own imprint on things, and if they are good, they add value. They, too, have sensitivities to the audience and are aware of what might produce the greatest impact if performed in the right manner.

We have two comments regarding the use of intermediaries. The first is that these intermediaries are called middle and upper-middle management in companies. They are the conveyors of representations. They are the ones who can transform a marvelous work into a thing of beauty or into a dud. Levels of ability will always exist throughout organizations, but you will always want those who are able to produce satisfying performances. Middle management, then, shouldn't be perceived as secondary players: they are fundamental to the entire work; and as just about anyone can attest based on experience, they are quite capable of engineering or ruining a good thing.

The second point is that talented intermediaries will want to put their individual mark on a performance without compromising the spirit of the work. We think this is a good thing, as it allows room for creativity and surprise. Classical composers, for example, left room in their compositions for improvisation that gave the performers allotted space to demonstrate their virtuosity. For example, it was fashionable during the classical period of music for composers to leave sections (the cadenza) of concertos blank, allowing the musicians to improvise based on prior content before being rejoined by the orchestra for the final coda.[2] Progress depends on variations, and companies will only get differences worth keeping if they encourage modest departures from the existing standards and conventions—if they permit little deviations from the master representation by allowing people to act autonomously. Every organization absolutely requires a talented center for sound execution, to facilitate change, and to improve.

# Chapter 6

# Imagination: Social Constructions and the Land of Make-Believe

**Question: Do I produce imaginative, original, and stimulating ways of conducting business, and have I created a company where inspired thinking thrives?**

*The motor car with its blinds drawn and an air of inscrutable reserve proceeded towards Piccadilly, still gazed at, still ruffling the faces on both sides of the street with the same dark breath of veneration whether for Queen, Prince, or Prime Minister nobody knew. The face itself had been seen only once by three people for a few seconds. Even the sex was now in dispute. But there could be no doubt that greatness was seated within; greatness was passing, hidden, down Bond Street, removed only by a hand's-breadth from ordinary people who might now, for the first and last time, be within speaking distance of the majesty of England, of the enduring symbol of the state which will be known to curious antiquaries, sifting the ruins of time, when London is a grass-grown path and all those hurrying along the pavement this Wednesday are but bones . . .*[1]

From *Mrs. Dalloway*, Virginia Woolf

Everything that is art as opposed to science occurs within a make-believe world. Great writers are especially adroit at manufacturing these worlds, which they invite us to inhabit. As much as we may try to resist being drawn in, or tell ourselves that what we are experiencing is make-believe, fiction writers and film directors get us to suspend our disbelief so that we may participate more fully in their drama. Think of the times that you have tried to withstand the terror produced by horror films by repeating to yourself, "It's only a movie, it's only a movie," but failed. The pensive quiet of a book or a darkened theater temporarily obliterates the world we know and replaces it with a new one: that of the artist.

A work of fiction isn't true, by definition. We know it isn't real, and so we don't rush on stage to save a king from ultimate doom or look for the characters of a book in the setting described on the pages. Yet we respond as if it were all real. One of us used to take our children to a wooded area across from our house in search of "the wild boar." They wanted to go on these adventures, which always yielded evidence of the boar (tracks, holes in trees that might be its home), but we never saw the boar itself. At dusk, with shadows stretching menacingly and the soft red glare of the setting sun reflecting off the nearby lake, the woods became a mysterious place where strange, wild creatures could dwell. To return home sweaty but still alive was always occasion for a seasonal celebration of hot chocolate or lemonade. If we were unable to feel the apprehension and fear, then we couldn't participate in the drama. Why, for example, protect oneself from a sneak attack by seeking out fresh prints if the wild boar did not exist *in this world*?

To make a story come alive, we have to imagine with the author that the place and people he or she describes are inherently logical and behave in certain credible ways. *Mrs. Dalloway* is a reflective self-study of a day in the inner life of the main character, Clarissa Dalloway. The premise for the action and parallel events is a party that Mrs. Dalloway is planning at her home, where the characters ultimately converge "like water round the piers of a bridge, drawn together." The book is full of subtlety and vivid descriptions, from a depiction of her friend Peter Walsh's confident and firm ordering of Bartlett pears in the hotel restaurant, which elicits a reaction from others nearby ("... they felt that he counted on their support in some lawful demand; was champion of a cause which immediately became their own ..."); to the description of the suicide of Septimus (a disturbed war veteran and counterpart to Mrs. Dalloway) by jumping from his apartment window ("Up had flashed the ground ..."); to the juxtaposition of life and death, with Mrs. Dalloway observing an old woman next door as party-goers occupy the adjacent room ("It was fascinating, with people still laughing and shouting in the drawing room, to watch the old woman, quite quietly, going to bed alone").

The longer passage we selected interests us because Woolf characterizes a scene in which we are asked to imagine people imagining who might occupy the magisterial car that is slowly passing by. She succeeds in transforming us, like the people on the pages, from passive bystanders to involved and inquisitive participants. Who is in the car? The scene works because we understand Woolf's constructed world, because it is a world that we have been a part of and is accessible to us. We've all stood on our toes to see what was happening beyond a sea of people and to glimpse at who might be passing by; we've wondered what the characters wonder, "Who is it?" "What is going on?" Woolf is able to draw us into her possible world because she is a great artist. There are many ways to convey meanings, but it is her irreplaceable way of saying it through the cadences and color of her prose that makes the difference. If the author wants us to imagine (and we must be willing to), she has to go well beyond the obvious, straightforward communication so we can picture ourselves chasing along with others after the car. The difference between great writers and the also-rans is that great writers use more sophisticated and refined methods of eliciting our imaginings and establishing a place where we can feel and understand the emotions and attitudes of the characters. Small differences in phrasing can entirely change our perspectives and responses. For example, imagine you are standing on a seaside cliff with a friend on a very windy day. The violent waves are pounding the rocks below. You say one of three things: "Imagine swimming in that," "Imagine yourself swimming in that," or "Imagine that you are swimming in that."[2] We leave it to you to determine if there are differences among these statements.

---

## THE COMPANY AS A SOCIAL CONSTRUCTION

We will start with what isn't always apparent, at least not in business. We create fictions: artificial environments. This makes it perfectly legitimate to ask, "If your company were a work of art, what would it look like?" It's really up to you. We don't think you need to turn your office complex into party central, but you have considerable room to put your imagination on display and avoid the "if you've seen one, you've seen them all" syndrome. If you were blindfolded and moved from company to company, each place would be nearly indistinguishable, and it would be hard to tell where you had landed.

For sport, and to counteract repetitive corporate environs, let's create a position called *chief imagination officer* (CImO). We are accustomed to creating different kinds of chiefs these days, so another won't hurt. How would the position description read?

The purpose of the chief imagination officer is to generate a total, integrated experience that fully absorbs people in the work of the organization and fosters creative thinking. The role of this job is to produce a credible illusory space that encourages originality in all aspects of work—methods, procedures, products, etc.—commensurate with the overall goals of the organization and consistent with its history and values, as if walking onto the pages of a book.

Before you dismiss this idea as hokey, think about all the times when you have been thoroughly engrossed in a game. The fact that you were playing didn't interfere with your ultimate aim: you wanted to win, and winning often required ingenuity between you and a partner to do so. The only difference is that at work, the CImO is the game manufacturer who is creating the rules of play and specifying how imaginative and how much fun he or she wants the game to be. We are not talking about diversions such as paddleball courts and massage rooms. The imaginative activity needs to encircle the goals of the organization. The activities can be simple things such as helping a product team that is knee deep in the big muddy get unstuck, or they can involve more permanent endeavors. Several years ago, we worked with a company that owned a baseball team and asked employees to vote on "all-star" employees by position, with original thinking as one of the criteria. The results (what else?) were printed on baseball cards with achievements printed on their backs.

We recently saw a company use a novel approach to talent management. Based on established criteria and management assessments, large squares that described strengths were created and laid on the floor. Managers were asked to stand on the squares that best represented their strengths, which instantaneously showed both a concentration of abilities in certain areas and clear deficits in others. The same exercise could have been done on paper, but then the company would most likely have missed out on the vigorous discussion that the live model produced and the collegial problem solving about succession that ensued.

As one final example, we once re-created a casino (for a company that operated casinos and resorts) and gave the executive team a fixed number of chips to use to place their bets on certain potential organizational initiatives. The accumulated bets that executives could allocate among several options provided an enhanced way to discuss group opinion. The virtue of the procedure is that a wide array of options were considered and independently weighed, yielding an instructive outcome that was achieved in a fun, evenhanded manner. The more we think about it, the more we are attracted to the idea of a CImO. If you think you have successfully tapped people's imaginative instincts, then perhaps the job we are proposing is unnecessary, but we think it is an intriguing idea just the same.

## Interference with Imagination

It is up to the leader to be imaginative and to inculcate imagination in others throughout the organization—excluding no one. We aren't asking for the fantastic from the leader, just things we have seen very good leaders do every day: formulate interesting alternatives and options within strategic boundaries, challenge the status quo, twist a question around so a new solution comes into view, reconceive the predominant business model, anticipate needs that others are unable to see, and so on. A leader has to have and democratically promote the generation of new ideas if his or her company is to get anywhere. Everyone reading this book can think of unimaginative leaders who despite mediocre results continue to do precisely the same things day in and day out—without new ideas or practices. Their great rescuer is the economy that occasionally turns in their favor, and they are saved by events outside their control. Some of the worst leaders, in our estimation, are not the ones who can't think resourcefully or boldly but the ones who don't because they insist that veering from standard protocols and orthodoxy is not permitted or somehow strangely unlawful. We cannot think of anything that cannot be improved upon in some fashion, hence, the need for imagination.

We assume that everyone has some capacity for imaginative thinking at work, although we have seen that the ability differs wildly among individuals, leaders included. With that presumption, there are still barriers to allowing imagination in. One is obvious: saying something that is different aloud can take guts. But here's what companies need to understand. People do in fact say ridiculous things, but we have seen clever people riff on those statements and turn them into something amazingly doable. We have seen half-jokes transformed in this same way. Leaders can create corporate cultures in which there are substantial tolerances for chancy utterances, far-fetched ideas, and mistakes.

There is, however, a much less obvious obstacle to imagination suggested in our example. Imagination requires a degree of immersion in the project at hand. It requires people to suspend belief in the world order so that minds can be occupied by the game at hand—the competitive match of business. Imagination comes from experience of something tangible, but people have to allow themselves to feel and breathe it all in. And there lies the problem. If a reader thinks, "I am reading a book that contains these unreal characters in familiar places that I know they have never been, experiencing things I know they have never seen or felt," then the book is ruined. Imagination requires attachment and an agreeableness of the enterprise. People who remain at arm's length, who never permit themselves to be participants but spectators only, will never be able to imagine, since that is specifically what they have chosen not to do. Engagement is essential to imagination: as in *Peter Pan*, the leader has to get the audience to clap in order to bring Tinkerbell back to life. If employees remain detached from the game and the fun it can offer, they won't be able to contribute in the same way as a person who has accepted the premises of imagination and is captivated in the Monopoly-esque events that occur in office towers throughout our cities.

## History and Imagination

The Latin root for imagination, *imago*, went through several meaning transformations. Before the fall of the Roman Empire, when burials versus cremations were the norm, imagoes were wax masks worn in funeral processions. The masks depicted the faces of the deceased's ancestors. With coins as tokens—needed for crossing the River Styx—encased with the deceased, we can imagine him or her joining family members in the underworld. The masks made it easier to imagine, but the fact that there were real ancestors with these likenesses made it *possible* to imagine. Imagination, then, requires a connection to the past that grounds our imaginative experiences and gives our beliefs plausibility. This is why we think that the preservation of corporate histories is vitally important and, even given a change in organizational direction, should never be completely abandoned. It is each person's link to the past that allows that individual to enter a speculative place and accept its possibilities. The Romans used imagoes, but companies have other means at their disposal to forge this connection. Some companies assign employee numbers as if in a processional from the first employee hired through to the most recent, e.g., "I'm employee number 224." Some companies we have seen use more symbolic mechanisms such as posting the names of patent holders and their associated innovations on a great wall as a means to underscore creativity, as is done in the adaptive specialty materials company Milligen & Co., a company that weathered the erosion of the traditional textile industry, reinvented itself, and is thriving.[3] Other companies have museums on their ground floors with artifacts from the company's history to illuminate special periods, inventions, and such. These are ways of personalizing the encounter and making all that follows more vibrant and real.

# Chapter 7

# Authenticity:
# Genuine Creations

**Question: Do I act in a manner that is true to my beliefs and that clearly articulates who I am and what I stand for?**

*The Supper at Emmaus*, Han van Meegeren
(Museum Boijmans Van Beuningen, Rotterdam. Loan: Museum Boijmans Van Beuningen Foundation. Photographer: Studio Tromp)

*The Milkmaid*, Johannes Vermeer
(Photograph: Getty Images)

Authenticity is one of those words with many synonyms (e.g., *genuine, real, original*) and antonyms (*fake, copy, imitation, forgery*). In this chapter, we have presented two images. The one on the right is of an authentic Vermeer, *The Milkmaid*. The one on the left is an infamous example of a forgery of a Vermeer, *The Supper at Emmaus*, painted in the 1930s by Han van Meegeren. This example is interesting because it is intended to replicate the style of Vermeer; it is not a reproduction of any of Vermeer's artworks.

Vermeer is undoubtedly one of the greats, but he was by no means prolific. In total, he created roughly 35 paintings, a marginal output compared with that of other masters. This may be attributable to the fact that he was an art dealer, innkeeper, and the father of 11 children. The finds of new Vermeers assuredly scintillated the art public, and the Dutch government tried to purchase as many of them as possible during the Second World War in order to preserve the Netherlands' cultural heritage and to keep the paintings from the grasp of the Nazis. However, van Meegeren had a fairly efficient fencing operation and one of the paintings (*The Woman Taken in Adultery*—we have seen it referenced by other names as well) was obtained by Hermann Goering in exchange for 127 paintings from his burgeoning wartime collection. Van Meegeren made a pretty good living selling faux Vermeers (about $3 million in today's dollars for *The Supper at Emmaus*) and other masters of an older era such as those purported to be works of Frans Hals and Pieter de Hoogh. Including *The Supper at Emmaus*, he sold at least six imitations of Vermeer and may have never been discovered had the painting he sold to Goering not been found in Goering's collection after the war. Rather than being tried for treason by the Dutch government, van Meegeren confessed to the forgery, which carried a much lighter penalty.

There were doubters about the legitimacy of the paintings at the time, but the point isn't that experts sometimes get fooled. The question is, "If it looks like a Vermeer, why can't we revere it like a Vermeer?" One reason is that a copy, stylistically or exact, adds nothing new to our understanding of art. For example, we believe that with the right materials and an art critic and chemist by our sides, we could reproduce an Albers with considerable fidelity. But what would be the point? A copy necessarily postdates the original, and when you have seen it before, there is nothing new to be seen. To the forger, one may rightly question and state: "Why don't you try to solve your own problems and come up with something that is your own? Something horribly yours may be better than a work that is expertly some else's."

Another reason we prefer to stand in front of the real Vermeer versus a forgery is because we appreciate the accomplishments of artists who are stylistically unique in a way that differentiates their art from that of another. Through the selection, treatment, and combination of artistic elements such as edges, textures, colors, surfaces, shapes, and so forth, we discover and applaud the person behind the art. We assign aesthetic value to works that are expressions of the artist's personal beliefs and to artists who act on what they genuinely mean and feel—and place much less weight on artists who ape the actions of others or who actively try to manipulate others without having their own personal commitment to what they do. We admire those who take risks and excel at the creative process. This is true in any discipline, whether entertainment, science, business, etc.

Therefore, reproductions don't command as much respect or attention. Harmless imitations that simply can be ignored become appalling when there is an intentional attempt to disguise the truth for self-interested purposes. Consider an example from Greek mythology. The frequently bored and always promiscuous Zeus, during one of his several conjugal visits to earth, disguised himself as the husband of Alcmene and seduced her. Although the husband and Zeus were indistinguishable, do you imagine that Alcmene was indifferent when she discovered the deception?[1] The answer is self-evident since we trust that our encounters with the arts or with one another are genuine. No matter how accurate and skillful the reproduction, we just don't respond the same way to fakes.

---

## ACCOMPLISHMENT

An important reason, then, that we prefer the real thing to fakes or reproductions is that individuality is embedded in the genuine article. Some value attaches itself to objects that are original. Regardless of what the marketplace has to say, we realize that an individual uniquely conceptualized the work, overcame obstacles, and realized the results. An authentic leader seeks out advice and contemplates options with others, but ultimately decides and initiates action on his or her authority, visualizing how events may unfold. The organization of a leader who is true to his or her beliefs has the fingerprint of its author throughout: the way it is designed, its culture, its value proposition. In addition, it can be said of an organization that is the product of an authentic leader, that it is peerless. It has a distinct status that attracts outsiders specifically because the company has ways in which it appeals to some types of people and not to others. One thing an authentic leader and his or her organization are *not* is boring.

Whether accomplishment consists of an *I* or a *we*, the common denominator is that someone did something out of the ordinary that others can appreciate as inspired. There are different things we admire in leaders aside from the direction they afford. We admire their tenacity and commitment to doing things right, according to personal convictions and beliefs. We applaud how they are able to meet challenges and persevere. We listen in awe as they weigh options and consider many conceivable alternatives. We watch them make do with limited resources, using them to maximum benefit. We witness their analytical prowess, originality, and compassion. Above all, we recognize those who, with the motivated hands of others, complete great works. The leader who achieves a one-of-a-kind performance, especially one that amazes for its ingenuity and distinctiveness, is someone who can be judged according to the merits he or she alone possesses. Others can replicate what was done if they wish, but it will never be theirs.

## Risk Taking

By definition, authenticity implies risk. When you copy, you are following a path that is known and worn. It is a safe path, and there will be no accolades for having taken the truest route available. Still, in most companies, the safest path is the easiest and most convenient to take. Even if the proven path later becomes the wrong path, it is an excusable error in most organizations, because it was the most evident course to take. Indeed, in many organizations, it will be taken again and again until the action is massively and noticeably absurd that it no longer can be ignored or forgiven. Until that time, however, although it may no longer be the most advantageous route, it remains the road most often taken because it has a built-in justification for its use. The choice liberates our journeymen from blame.

In fact, we would go so far as to say that organizations breed homogeneity or, at most, the slightest deviations, since past successes tend to be rewarded and replicated. It is very hard for leaders and employees to break free from the established mold. The old saw that it is easier to ask for forgiveness than for permission is a lovely saying if you want to die poor. What most people end up learning from their mistakes is not to make them, and that most often entails playing it safe—even if it means walking in an errant, but conventional, direction. And this is why artists and great leaders are heroes in our society. They deserve to be, because they stand apart from the crowd by the work they believed in and the risks they knowingly took. They will be remembered at the extremes by history for their great successes or sensational flops. For good or bad, they tried.

## Keeping It Personal

The old trickster Zeus helps us to see not only what authenticity means to others, but what it should mean to you when people try to pass off your creation as their own: when they replicate and present something that is yours as if they were the real progenitor. There is little else that is more reprehensible than feigning an achievement that belonged to another. It is the worst kind of theft: being robbed of a performance as opposed to a possession, a lost form of ownership that is far more personal and precious than a commodity. The latter you can purchase again at another time. The accomplishment improperly assigned and so highly prized is gone forever.

There are countless instances of credit taken where it wasn't due. We can say that the leader who snatches what is rightfully yours cannot be a leader of merit. Indeed, we can say with certitude that your career is not high on the leader's list. The employee caught in such a scenario has options ranging from an amended report from the boss to inclusion of his or her instrumental role of the accomplishment in the yearly performance review. The best option, however, is to get out of Dodge and find a more respectable leader who cares about your success and advancement. A great leader not only hones his or her own abilities, but enables and marvels at the good work of others, nurturing them as their talents warrant. The leader's job is to help others become successful, not to falsely inflate or attribute accomplishments to themselves.

## Lack of Commitment

There are many problems with forgers, but a contender for one of the largest is their lack of sincerity. Forgers have no convictions of their own. They will do what it takes to get what they want. For Zeus, it was the fair maiden. For van Meegeren, it was a bit of notoriety as an eminent dealer, but mostly it was the money. Behind every creation is a lie. Artists who dispassionately produce replicas of works have no belief system of their own—at least none that can be detected from their work. It is the same with leaders. Those who simply copy the work of others are hard to decipher, since they don't reveal anything about themselves through their works. Without a reinforcing ideation voiced with zeal, we are left with the empty words of a leader and his or her shallow, transient commitments. These leaders lose their constituency by failing to take a stand. They flirt with the latest fads and are easily seduced by fashionable, but fleeting, ideas. They have no firm beliefs and, therefore, give us nothing in their work to believe in. Frequently, ungrounded and unburdened by values, these people, these forgers, are manipulators. They will urge action, sometimes fervently even if falsely, if it gets them what they want for themselves. It would be accurate to call such leaders frauds, since these people fail to meet their own standards of correctness, if they happen to have any such standards at all.

We connect to one another by being authentic and steadfast in our convictions. It is the foundation of many different types of close relationships, including those involving leaders and followers. Who wants to follow people who don't know what they believe in or stand for? Or sometimes worse, who wants to follow people who constantly change their minds or send out contradictory messages? Expressing what you think and following through in myriad ways is what a leader does. You won't always win converts to your cause, simply because what you say truthfully may not resonate with some. However, for those who accept a leader's commitments as their own, the leader will have won what may be most essential to the organization's success, the followers' allegiance.

## Kitsch Management

One type of fraud deserves special mention. We call it kitsch management after a type of art that is expressly made to produce predictable emotional reactions. It is a form of art that is cheap, superficial, and manipulative. The word *kitsch* comes from the German, and one translation is "to play with mud." Therefore, kitsch might be thought of as a method of management that intentionally mucks with one's emotions. Kitsch does its dirty work through iconic imagery or caricatures to which we are conditioned—to which we affectively respond—because of the associations we naturally make. For example, we might associate cute, fluffy kittens with domestic warmth and tranquillity, the national flag with patriotism, and the cross with religious convictions. In all these cases, you are being led somewhere—not by the object itself but by what the object usually represents. It is possible for home wreckers, traitors, and atheists to deploy these symbols because they know how people are likely to react even if they don't subscribe to the positions the artifacts represent.

A little trivia and drivel are harmless; we would even say that, at times, they are welcome diversions from the more heady stuff in our lives. (Besides, we are talking about kitsch art, not popular art, which is different: we happen to like much of the latter and don't consider ourselves snobs when it comes to the mass appeal of objects that often are summarily dismissed as artistically unworthy.) We are opposed to exploitation and the use of deceitful methods to get one's way. In essence, we dislike what psychologists call Machiavellianism. The cunning of Machiavellianism is richer in its deceits than the use of symbolism alone, but the use of symbols is one way to squelch dissent and preserve the status quo: to retain power. Uniforms, corporate pins, the hierarchical arrangement of office space, mahogany paneling, and so on are all symbols that, in the wrong hands, can be used to convey the idea that employees who want to be good team players should never question the leadership—in other words, do what you are told, don't make waves, and everything will be all right.

# Chapter 8

# Engagement:
# The Curious Culture

**Question: Do I produce a challenging and intellectually stimulating environment where people feel compelled to take on issues and work hard to generate solutions?**

*Las Meninas*, Diego Velázquez
(Photograph: Corbis Images)

The best works of art are the ones that people are able to return to with sustained interest. There is always something new to see and to contemplate. Great art in any medium is able to repeatedly draw you in and force you to seek out its embodied meaning through careful examination and discovery. The Velázquez painting on display in this chapter is one of the most vexing works in art history. It was a hit at the time it was painted (as a commissioned work of the monarch) and still is today. If any work has astonished and withstood the test of time, this is surely one of them. In addition, few paintings have been studied more than this one, which enchants viewers with a single, elusive question: "What is Velázquez trying to say?" The painter presumably places what we need to know in front of us, but we must work out for ourselves what he is attempting to relate. This is far from the self-evident and superficial kitsch in which cuddly kittens or tearful little boys are unambiguously portrayed. If we aren't driven to do some work of our own, it usually is not art.

Unfortunately, today will not be the day when we solve the riddle of *Las Meninas*. We use it to show that if the artist has to tell us everything, the art isn't as much fun. People have to figure some things out for themselves: indeterminacy and people's natural inclinations for investigation and discovery account for a great deal of the pleasure of art.

Everyone in *Las Meninas* is a real person of the court of Philip IV and Queen Mariana (wife and niece of the king), although, absent furniture, the scene is clearly artistically contrived. One of the central figures in the painting is the Infanta princess who later marries King Leopold of Germany. This is an unusual portraiture for the time, since portraits weren't ordinarily rendered in group settings as this one is. The princess is attended by two handmaidens, the *meninas*, both of whom were considered aristocrats of the Castilian family tree. The light from the window illuminates the Infanta, but a smattering of sun partly shines on the other central figure in the painting, the artist himself, who strikes a pose similar to one he painted of Saint John years before. The gaze of the characters tends to be outward, and one presumes that the king and queen are in their company. Just where they are situated is a matter of conjecture. Critics have gone so far as to measure angles, and one belief is that the reflection of the king and queen at the back of the room is coming from the large canvas before the artist, and not from the actual king and queen, who may have been moving about the room or changing their positions.

Above the mirror are two paintings that were a part of the royal court's inventory and that, interestingly, Velázquez decided to use in his painting. They are derivatives of works by Rubens. Both works depict tussles between gods and mortals, with the latter not faring well in either. The one on the left depicts a weaving contest between Minerva and Arachne, and the one on the right, a musical contest between Apollo and Pan. Arachne ends up as a spider, and while Pan isn't punished, King Midas, who protests the ruling of Apollo as winner, has his ears transformed into those of an ass to reflect his lack of discernment in music. First, Velázquez appears to be inferring, "I have to be very careful here and not overstep court conventions," despite the fact that he was friendly with the king, who visited the painter's studio within Alcázar Palace often. Indeed, the very fact that it is Velázquez's head that is highest in the work would have been reason for trepidation, since it is the king's power that must be on display (but the king isn't *really* in the picture; this picture within a picture ad infinitum is called the Droste effect and wasn't atypical for the period). Second, the paintings on the back wall are knock-offs of works by Rubens that juxtapose tapestry and music: at the time, painting was considered an inferior, mechanical art akin to weaving, while music had attained higher status as a fine art. In addition to suggesting that the craft of painting should be on a par with music, Velázquez may be unobtrusively mocking the king's taste or voicing his displeasure with the king's unwillingness to give a mortal, Velázquez, his due: Velázquez ambitiously hoped to join the aristocracy and had wanted the king to knight him as he had Rubens! Even the minor players in the painting such as the dwarfs, who occupied the palace in abundance, seemed to have had higher standing: they were like court jesters with liberties that would have been the death of others.

Overall, the work may be interpreted as a celebration of the painter-artist and a subtle means for Velázquez to voice his innermost desire to join the aristocracy. Three years after the completion of this painting (1656) and eight months before his death, Velázquez received his hard-won honor and became a Knight of Santiago.

## KEEP WANTING MORE

Most good art keeps you coming back for more. There is something about it—its sensuality, its grandeur, its mystery—that entrances and stimulates repeated returns to the work in order to reach satisfying conclusions to nagging questions left unanswered: "How did he produce that effect?" "Why did he include this object in the painting versus another like it?" "What determined the size of the work?" Our illustration is one of the great puzzlers of all time, and we use it as an extreme example of what art does: it gets you to think. The artist has done his or her part, and it is up to you to do the rest.

In a word, art *engages*. Engagement has become a popular meme in business; it broadly defines a person's motivation and strength of connection to the organization. But to what end? We think the artist has something more specific in mind for our leaders. The artist wants to present problems that will tap in to an individual's natural inquisitiveness. Engagement means having employees who are invested in solving the organization's most demanding dilemmas by repeatedly exploring the evidence until solutions are conceived or discovered.

## Curiosity

We once knew a CEO who held quarterly staff meetings that were billed as mini States of the Union. The only problem was that there were never any facts or analyses presented. It was mostly an occasion for undeserved self-congratulation. The quarterly meetings that were designed to be uplifting events were creatively fallow and demoralizing. There was nothing to think about. If attendance were not mandatory, the hall surely would have been empty. Instead, the meetings became fare for ridicule.

People are fundamentally curious, but they have to be given something that piques their curiosity. Executives shouldn't presume to have all the answers—they certainly can't know all the questions. Something has to be left for people to figure out on their own. Otherwise, what is the value of employees if you ask them to leave their brains at the door? Present employees with questions: "Why did sales of a certain product suddenly drop off this month?" "Why isn't our product gaining market share despite equivalent quality to the competitor and a lower price point?" "Why are we experiencing above-normal quality problems in one of our plants?" If you never present questions and insist on having all the answers, the result will be the opposite of what you want from a workforce: silence. Curiosity will be quashed. Many times people will offer answers that have already been thought about and tested, but that isn't a waste of time. We would call it engagement.

At the other extreme, which we applaud, is Irwin Simon, the CEO of Hain Celestial Group, the organic and natural foods and products company, who has an open door policy for meetings.[1] In order to stimulate questions, learn about other parts of the company, and be better informed, anyone can go into any meeting. The door is always considered open. Simon has been known to bring interns into board meetings so that they can become accustomed to the sorts of discussions that occur in those settings and become comfortable expressing their opinions in such high-profile situations.

## Going on a Hunt

Engagement isn't just insular: it is an extracurricular matter as well. It involves being integrated into the professional community so that one can search for answers outside the confines of the corporate walls. Whatever the true answer is to the Velázquez painting, it isn't to be found just in the work of art. We can see the prominence of the artist, but had we not known about his long-standing desire to join a military order and the aristocracy, many aspects of the painting would have been difficult to interpret. "Even the lowly keeper of the tapestries [the person standing in the back doorway in the painting] has a more privileged position than I," we might hear him mutter. Thus, to remain engaged inside the organization, the leader has to make sure people are engaged outside the organization. Otherwise, all answers will be restricted to what is internally observable and already known. External involvement might include attending conferences, visiting the facilities of noncompetitors, going to trade shows, taking classes, and so on as time and money permit. One of the worst things a company can do is become insular and closed-minded. The company may ride a wildly successful product for a while, but without a steady influx of new ideas, it sooner or later will falter. For example, it has been suggested that Nokia's recent fall in market share partly was a result of its isolation from web and consumer electronics companies, and so it was not inclined to challenge assumptions about its products.[2]

## Getting Engagement

The clearest way to get engagement is, first, to present facts that people can see and reflect upon. We are not necessarily advocating open-book management although we are both proponents of it. The problems presented to employees can be more piecemeal and exacting. They can be of the ilk, "Look at this graph; it shows a trend that we don't quite understand . . ." As the co-owners of the Business Literacy Institute, Karen Berman and Joe Knight astutely point out that what your employees don't know can be quite harmful to your company. For example, plant managers who are unaware of rising returns and warranty expenses may be tempted to use subpremium parts to lower production costs, or engineers who are in the dark about tight cash flow and thin cash reserves may be busy designing products with new features that the company will not be able to afford and manufacture.[3] Second, the problem has to have a baseline of complexity. It should be nuanced and interesting, and its resolution ought to have substantial implications for the department, unit, or company. Third, the leader has to build a culture of inquisitiveness, allowing people the freedom to think for themselves. Some companies set up problems around the premises for people to look at and study. Implicit in this arrangement is that there is no limited admission to thinking. Everyone shares in the problems, and everyone is responsible for the solutions. Along these lines, we like a quote attributed to Andy Grove, the former head of Intel: to paraphrase, if you don't know who is responsible, assume it's you.

## Tact and Diplomacy

There are times when it will be difficult to make suggestions, and there will be sensitive issues that will be hard to broach. In Velázquez's day, a little mistake could be fatal despite the fact that the king liked the artist. Life at the top was precarious, and the king always had to be protective of his stature and might. *Las Meninas* was painted with the king's consent for the king himself: any implication of contempt or diminution of standing would be, let's say, frowned upon. So Velázquez painted an unlikely portrait of the Infanta, with the king and queen as mere reflections; and he painted the artist, of course, as notably noble. It was a high-wire act, and the artist probably knew it. Ever so slyly, he communicated that the noblest person in the room was in fact treated as the least noble. If the king got the message that he was slighting the court painter, he didn't show it since Velázquez carried on at the palace until his death from natural causes. Intellectual engagement doesn't mean, then, the end of tact; nor does it mean long discourses on who is right and who is wrong, who is smart and who is not. CEOs who make decisions within the boundaries of propriety are always right in their own way, but you still need to be able to tell them when they are wrong. Wise CEOs will know how to listen to the prudently expressed opinions of trusted employees and advisors.

# Chapter 9

# Pleasure: Emotional Nourishment and Personal Enrichment

**Question: Do I produce an enriching and satisfying environment where people are able to thrive and grow?**

Untitled (*Sculptural Study, Five-Part Construction*), Fred Sandback (Photograph by Yotam Hadar, http://www.yotamhadar.com)

*The Vietnam Veterans Memorial*, Maya Lin (Photograph: Getty Images)

What makes art distinctly satisfying apart from life's many other pleasures has a lengthy history. The debate rages on, and we are poorly equipped to resolve the controversy. But there are two things we can say with reasonable confidence. First, art should supply pleasure in myriad ways: it should be valuable, admirable, illuminating, awesome, enjoyable, and subjectively savory. Said more directly, it should be distinguishable from blatantly hedonistic pleasures such as, say, a massage or an episode of *Two and a Half Men*.

Second, much of the pleasure in art resides in personal involvement and direct participation. If you have ever witnessed the spontaneity of a mob dance, then you have seen firsthand the joy that involvement in artistic practice can bring—some of it well choreographed and quite striking in terms of mass and movement. Many forms of art rely on participation in order to be fully appreciated. Often, these are instances of public art. They include decorative open spaces such as piazzas, stunningly beautiful architecture such as churches, and monuments and memorials. To take in the full power of the art, you have to engage with it and with others present in ways prescribed by the art itself. Churches invite solemnity, prayer, songs of praise, and holy celebration, all performed as a collective.

One of our examples does not elicit the rapture of architecturally beautiful houses of worship and associated religious ceremonies, but evokes a range of emotions from gratitude, to sorrow, to pride, to loss. Mix them together, and you take a reverential walk with others down the incline of The Vietnam Veterans Memorial, in our estimation one of the great works of public art. Pleasure isn't a unidimensional concept, and we aren't unidimensional creatures—and The Vietnam Veterans Memorial is a testament to that. We would define the experience we are talking about broadly as pleasure, but of a kind that is more enduring and poignant than the transient pleasures we pass through daily. What gives these elite satisfactions their distinction is that they incorporate our most basic and cherished ideals and values into their affective fabric. The memorial appropriately doesn't produce the raw joys that management consultants tend to think about and promote in organizations, but people keep coming back, and they wouldn't if the work weren't rewarding in some way. Clearly the pleasure experienced isn't one of ecstasy, but of satisfying a yearning to recognize sacrifice and courage. Despite the deaths it commemorates, the memorial appeals to values that we admire and duly pays its respect to the people who exemplify those values. It isn't upbeat by any means; it is nourishing.

As a great work of art, it achieves its effects through complete engagement of body and soul. Briefly, if you want to experience the work as it is intended to be experienced, you must first descend the fissure in the earth. The 58,106 names of the dead are organized chronologically, not alphabetically. The first killed start in the middle and work up to one end: the names then continue back in the middle on the other side of the apex of the memorial and work up the other side: down, up, down, up. The center of the piece is the nadir of a 10-foot decline—to us, there has always been an uneasy feeling of joining the dead. But the glossy-faced granite with your image superimposed on the names, along with the reflections of others, brings you back to a life that is renewed by an overwhelming sense of gratitude to those who have given so much to give us so much. Flowers are laid at the base. Aging parents make rubbings of the names of their sons; people silently and somberly communicate with one another with knowing glances. It is one of the most moving works on the planet, and certainly not without its controversy at the time. But it has more than proved its worth to generations.

The other artistic work is a modernist piece by Fred Sandback, which offers quite a different rendering of artistic pleasure. Sandback's sculptures are an integration of simple materials such as yarn of various thicknesses that are stretched from ceiling to floor or from wall to wall, giving the illusion of virtual glass panes. His pieces are site-specific in dimension and in the way they relate to the space: again, nothing that an artist of Sandback's stature does is accidental. There is a reason for everything.

The shapes provide the appearance of three-dimensional objects and surfaces such as in the example: the yarn configurations look like sheets of glass, and it would be fair to describe these panes as the art of absence. What is fun about his work is that people don't know what to do with it. They look intently at it, and like it, but they are confused about how to interact with it. Does one walk through a virtual pane of glass or around it? It forces people to work through how they are going to relate to the art, to the space, and with each other. It reminds us of Tavistock groups where people interact without any clear objective—people have to figure out the emptiness on their own and, in so doing, reveal something about themselves. Sandback's work is the artistic parallel of people trying to negotiate their presence with imaginary floating objects. It is pure, wholesome enjoyment.

---

## A Special Kind of Pleasure

If we could not feel, there would be no art. Indeed, if we couldn't feel, we suspect that we wouldn't care about leadership either. If neither art nor leadership produced meaningfully heightened pleasures, then neither would have lasting human appeal. What would be the point? One of the things that set us apart as a species is our capacity to feel. If our leaders generated limp, flat, affectively neutral experiences, two things would result. First, we would not fully understand what they were saying, because how we emotionally respond to utterances and events provide us with indispensable clues to their meaning: nor would we care what they had to say, since there would be no reward in it. Second, since we would feel blasé, our own urge for expression would be muted. We would have a society of pod people. Could a body snatcher create art or lead effectively when the sine qua non for creative insight is emotion? If a thumbtack or plastic garbage pail produces the same level of excitement as the leader, something is terribly wrong.

As our examples illustrate, emotive reactions to what leadership presents need not be uniformly positive. But they can't obliterate hope and optimism either. As The Vietnam Veterans Memorial shows, it is possible to take a tragedy and make it into something that changes our outlook for the better. We can't alter or hide the circumstances, but a great leader will enable us to discover the virtues that are present and maintain our confidence in the future. A great leader will, following the art critic and philosopher, Monroe Beardsley, keep people whole: enabling a sense of integration and a feeling of being restored—a hearty contentment that includes self-acceptance and self-expansion as fundamental components.[1]

## Hands On

Sometimes people are nourished by intellectual challenges, like a puzzle that sustains their attention until the solution is found. However, at other times, there is an inherent pleasure in handling things. It is the forgotten sensory experience: touching. It is one of the ways people learn: for example, by gaining an intimacy with a machine and how its constituent parts fit together. One of the most enjoyable elements of consulting is watching monster machines doing their work and people adroitly exploiting the machines' capacities. In the world of the virtual, avatars, and the cloud, we may be losing some of the tactile aspects of work and our ability to innovate as we lose our "feel" for things—particularly as we watch manufacturing disappear and more production being outsourced abroad. There is pleasure in generating and holding an elegant report, but these mostly are treated as dispensable, consumable goods—and as purely utilitarian. If there are ways to make office work more tangible, we would recommend it. One way is to get out of the office and visit where the goods are made and tested. Seeing, smelling, and touching are ways to feel more connected to, and less estranged from, the work to which employees' efforts contribute. A central part of the experience of The Vietnam Veterans Memorial is being able to touch it and trace the name of a loved one onto a sheet of paper. The encounter wouldn't be the same if it weren't close. Similarly, it is part of the leader's job to make the intangible more real, lest employees remain distant, as if hugging the edge of the memorial walkway and being uninvolved in the production and consequences of their work. Leaders can't afford to have people sitting in the stands, observing versus participating, as events materialize.

## Participation

There are two interesting observations about the Sandback piece with respect to business. First, the space itself is naturally interesting and invites thoughtfulness and exploration. There is nothing fancy about the way he did it. He tended to use everyday industrial materials in his sculptures and designs. A part of the pleasurable experience of work is having a work area that is pertinent and fun. There is now ample proof that how the insides of buildings are designed and laid out affects our moods, our thoughts, and our health. However, the idea isn't to produce whimsy for the sake of it. You are trying to invent a vibrant environment that achieves a few things:

1. Showcases the creative output of the organization; e.g., these can be garments, books, gadgets, toys (for toy manufacturers), scale models, and other accoutrements that depict the creative punch of the company—and that also can be physically handled. The web-based company Etsy trades in handmade arts and crafts and

lives by the motto "Stay handmade." Consequently, employees receive hand-carved desks and a $100 allowance to decorate their offices using found and crafted objects and materials. The offices reflect the goods they purvey.[2]

2. Produces a work setting that underscores the cultural imperatives of the organization in original ways, replacing the usual placards and sales figures that are posted on walls; e.g., walking through the corridors of a prestigious academic institution, you will notice what is important through the way the halls are decorated—with research reports that at once convey the importance of research but also communicate the open exchange of ideas. Or walk through WET Design, where CEO Mark Fuller wants designers to post their ideas on the walls to make them available for critique as well as to highlight the norm that an open, honest exchange of ideas is essential to corporate success.[3]

3. Invites spontaneous interactions among people and active participation within a collegial atmosphere. The illustrative works suggest that individuals get the most from their daily experiences when they are involved in enlightening or exhilarating social encounters. Sandback's piece demonstrates art's ability to foster meaningful interactions even (or especially) among people with dissimilar backgrounds; e.g., they are from different disciplines and departments. The visitors to a Sandback sculpture, for instance, have never met before and yet they fondly interact.

The second illustrative point for business is less perceptible. The participatory nature of the art is most effective when people enter art's range with similar attitudes. Art-goers have their individual outlooks and beliefs, but in art's domain they assemble with a common cause: to appreciate, in some fashion, whether to collectively figure out a maze constructed from household materials or to console one another for a nation's loss. If you want a prime example of how uncommon causes work, just look back to the end of 2011 and see how the super 12 from Congress performed to balance our national budget: if you recall, divisively and poorly. Participation works when people realize that they are all in it together. For Sandback's art, that means mutually trying to decipher the meaning of his work and what constitutes appropriate behavior within its space. The experimentation proceeds in a playful manner, with some people poking their hands through the "glass"; some, who have construed the yarn shapes as mirrors, positioning themselves on each side of the "mirror" and mimicking one another's movements; and some wandering around and through the imaginary partitions and entranceways, carrying on as a joyous ensemble. We long for those leaders who can reproduce the spontaneity and sense of community that art has the power to create.

## Aesthetic Health and Leadership Dropouts[4]

We have a tendency in business to think of leaders as getting other people sufficiently motivated to act on the company's objectives with at least a modicum of vigor. But people will only participate and act if they have not lost their capacity to engage in the enterprise and appreciate a good chunk of what the leader and life have to offer. If they are no longer receptive to the work of others and cannot appreciate beauty in its various forms, then they have abdicated a life of meaning for easy pleasures and selective solitude. These people have given up on themselves, concluding that there is nothing profound worth their time to pursue and that no expansive inquiry can rekindle the light that has been spent. They won't enter Sandback's spaces, nor will they allow themselves to be absorbed or overwhelmed by the monumental messages of The Vietnam Veterans Memorial. They have no desire to lead or be led, because they have lost what is essential to each: an interest in a contemplative life and a belief that they are creative, efficacious human beings. They convince themselves that they could if they would (produce something of substance and meaning), but elect not to, thereby protecting their self-ascribed shortcomings and telling themselves they have better things to do. In this regard, we are reminded of Melville's scrivener, Bartleby, who frustrates his employer by saying, "I prefer not to," in response to each request—all of which are reasonable and well-intentioned.[5]

Poor Bartleby. Not everyone can be saved, but it is the leader's job to keep people alive by preserving their intellectual and emotional health and sustaining their passion, so that they never figuratively drop out of the workforce. The way to keep people interested is to produce an engaging work environment that promotes rich interactions, contains alluring projects, and is welcoming of their participation and contributions. Foremost, the leader's job is to maintain the convictions of all employees that they are capable and have something of importance to offer. We have met far too many people in organizations who have stopped trying.

# Chapter 10

# Human Significance: Why Art and Leadership Persist

**Question: Am I able to build a community that is cemented by basic human needs and concerns?**

*The True Artist Helps the World by Revealing Mystic Truths (Window or Wall Sign),* 1967 (neon tubing with clear glass tubing suspension frame, 59 × 55 × 2 inches [149.9 × 139.7 × 5.1 cm])
(Photograph courtesy Sperone Westwater, New York. Philadelphia Museum of Art: Purchased with the Henry P. McIlhenny Fund, the bequest [by exchange] of Henrietta Meyers Miller, the gift [by exchange] of Philip L. Goodwin, and contributions from generous donors, 2007. © Bruce Nauman/ Artists Rights Society [ARS], New York)

Ｗe know from the cave drawings in Lascaux, France, that making art is at least 15,000 years old, and it certainly precedes that date by a long shot (evidence suggests by another 30,000 years). Surely we were dancing by the time we became exclusively bipedal. It is legitimate to wonder why people on the fringes of survival would take the time to paint their walls. They did though, and these primitive cultures were not undone by the ravages of too much art and not enough hunting and gathering. And millennia later, here we are: where every culture continues to produce art. We think the Bruce Nauman piece on display as our example helps to explain why.

This particular piece by Nauman is one of his better known in a series in which he questions the role of the artist in society, and his own identity as an artist. In equating artists to those who reveal mystic truths, there is good reason to believe that this work is satirical when juxtaposed with other, similar works. The probing question is genuine, but Nauman's answer, we suspect, is betrayed in works in which he compares artists to luminous fountains. One work we particularly have in mind is called *The True Artist is an Amazing Luminous Fountain*; the words of the work's title are inscribed on a transparent, rose-colored Mylar shade that is hung over a window. The viewer is forced to look at the wording on the shade and, in so doing, must reflect on the artist as the generative source of one's vision. What the observer sees instead, however, is nothing but the outdoors. The same inscription has been hung around door frames, again suggesting that what is to be seen beyond the words is what is already there. The artist is simply making more visible what is in front of us but overlook, and what we know but fail to think deeply enough about.

These works remind us that great art is grounded in the everyday, and that artists have no special faculty for ultimate truths or unique religious insights. In casting artists as mystics or luminous fountains, Nauman is playing with our conventional notions of artists as creative geniuses who produce transcendental worlds that are unavailable to the rest of us. At most, art helps us to imagine possible worlds with possible people in them based on what we see, know, and want. If we didn't understand and appreciate art at a highly personal level, we would have no use for it, and it never would have flourished through the ages. It would have been extinguished as an intriguing but immaterial experiment in the evolution of humankind.

The historical practice and preservation of art requires that it maintain an intimate connection to our earthly needs. Art has survived across time and societies because it provides insights that are not above us, as we sometimes imagine, but are aimed directly at us. The needs that art satisfies are those that allow us to live richer, more reflective lives, and to form stronger social ties more subtly and powerfully than we would at a group sing of the national anthem.

Why did our great, great ancestors paint animals on cave walls? Didn't they know there were perfectly good animals lurking around outside? The Mylar shade in Nauman's *Luminous Fountain* piece suggests that a critical value of art is its ability to show us something—the ordinary outdoors—in a different light. It forces us to examine our feelings, beliefs, interests, and values, not in order to reveal new, great mystic truths but to uncover old ones that make our lives special and worth living. Quite frequently, we share similar experiences and reactions to art as others: these emotional connections draw us closer together. We hunger for these affinities because we want to share with others those things that give us pleasure and have meaning. We want others to like the books and movies we like, for example, so that for a while we are able to occupy a common space in which we both take delight. That convergence of feelings and experiences builds communities.

We don't know what the cave drawings meant to our human predecessors, but we know this for sure: they meant something, or else they never would have been created. Perhaps the drawings conveyed the skill and courage of the hunt, or a divine presence in nature that provided an ample supply of food, or thankfulness to their maker for a good week in the field. Whatever they felt, they felt it together. At least some members of the group understood and appreciated the drawings in the same way. The art per se may not be adaptive, but building a unified community certainly is.[1]

We can't think of anything more profound than an activity that asks us to explore our priorities and values, examine the kind of lives we wish to live, and discover others' tastes and interests that are most congenial to our own. When we want to separate, we send in the army. When we want to unite, we send in the musicians. Recently, a Karachi-based ensemble (Qawal Najmuddin Saifuddin & Brothers) that performs 700-year-old Sufi devotional music (*qawwali*) toured the United States.[2] The group's mission was to introduce American audiences to a brand of Islamic traditional music and to build bridges between cultures that have had a hard time understanding each other through more conventional political means. When all else fails, art survives. It survives because it addresses what is common to all of us: our shared humanity.

-----

## FOUNTAIN MANAGEMENT

We think it is revealing that the title of Nauman's work, *The True Artist is an Amazing Luminous Fountain*, could be changed to *The True Leader is an Amazing Luminous Fountain*, and remain equally provocative. As our headliner image implies, both statements are questions about the purpose of artists and leaders, and whether they are the originators of arcane truths. Both statements borrow on the use of the word *fountain*. On the one hand, a fountain denotes wisdom and uncanny knowledge. On the other hand, fountains have been useful symbols of irony, connoting neither light nor truth. In fact, even Nauman facetiously pokes fun at artists as wellsprings of clairvoyance in a self-portrait in which he shows himself spitting out water. In a more recent work, *Venice Fountain*, hollow-cast heads (numbskulls?) spew recycled water. We take the metaphor of a fountain a step further. Rather than view know-it-all leaders as above reproach, we suggest that the allusion to a fountain may divulge the dangerousness of such conceits. The most famous fountain in the arts is Duchamp's urinal, dated 1917. It has been conceived as a derisive commentary on Europe's false grandeur, arrogance, and pomposity, which ultimately cost the lives of over 15 million people.

Several years ago, a group of us went to Rome. Each of us had to become an expert on some aspect of the art and architecture of Rome and explain it to one another. We selected Gian Lorenzo Bernini. Bernini was a fortunate choice since one of his masterworks was his *Fountain of Four Rivers* located in the urban square Piazza Navona—one of the great hangouts in the world, which afforded plenty of opportunity to play expert. The Piazza Navona is a former stadium that once seated 15,000 people who enjoyed chariot races and other athletic contests during the reign of Domitian. The Pamphili family bought the land, built a mansion that housed a future pope (Innocent X) and other family members, and commissioned a centerpiece befitting the family name. Bernini did not win the bid (in fact, because of his association with the prior pope, Urban VIII, he wasn't even asked to bid since Pope Innocent X wanted to distance himself from the extravagances of the former pope—unsuccessfully, we might add) but managed to obtain it anyway through insider influence.

Many speculate it was the evil sister-in-law that influenced the pope by judiciously placing a scale model of Bernini's plans in front of him. Even though it was commissioned by the leader of the Catholic Church and is truly a grand piece, it is entirely a secular ornament of familial opulence and a display of power. It shows the unification of the world through four river gods that represented the four continents of the known world. In the center is an Egyptian obelisk unearthed by the Romans in the first century AD and brought back to Rome. The obelisk would have both exemplified past Roman glory and conquest and instilled mystery due to the undeciphered hieroglyphs on it. The work is topped by the family seal, a dove with an olive branch. At the time the work was completed, a time of famine, this is where many in the city would have gathered to obtain their drinking water. This fountain, then, quenched physical needs as well as the rapacious psychological needs of the ruling family. The creative, flourishing spirit of a fountain is juxtaposed with the fatal leadership flaws of invincibility and omniscience. To summarize, leaders who earnestly consider themselves to be amazing and luminous, and who believe that they are uncannily in touch with hidden truths, think far too highly of, and seriously about, themselves. They are at best unhelpful and at worst terrifying (see Francis Bacon's alarming portrait of Innocent X).

## Leadership Reflection

If leaders don't have anything special to offer people, then why lead? It is this self-reflexive question that lies beneath much of the work that Nauman has done over the years. Why am I an artist? What is it that artists do? What function am I fulfilling? A part of the answer is that the artist must have fun doing it and receive enough positive feedback that the effort seems worthwhile. However, assuming one's purposes are noble, why do artists make art or leaders lead in the first place? They have to. The artist and the leader have an irrepressible urge to make a personal statement that they consider to be important enough to express and share with others. These statements derive importance from the concerns that reside in everyday life: exceptionally made articulations of universal concerns as contrasted with the rambling fantastical musings of blowhards.

As in looking through an unusual pane of glass, a true leader asks people to consider anew what has always been in front of them. The artist-leader invites you to think about basic earthly questions such as "How do you want to think about yourself?" "What kind of person do you want to be?" "What is it that you really want?" "What is your opinion about XYX?" "Do you think that you have exhausted your potential, or can you do more, better?" The success or failure of a leader many times hinges on getting people to think about these very questions at critical moments—when there are decisions about right and wrong to be made. Indeed, we believe that many cases of obvious misdeeds are traceable to a leader's inability to break through unreflective, self-serving, and mindless decisions in preference to more thoughtful and self-aware actions. We would call that failure, gross mismanagement.

Videos that document the 2011 pepper-spraying incident at UC Davis undoubtedly are still available on the web. If you somehow missed it, we recount it for you here: Sit-in student protestors lined themselves across a campus street, blocking passage. The campus police were given orders to remove them, and they used pepper spray to incapacitate the students before forcible removal. The methodical spraying is a bit unnerving to watch. Apart from a number of management miscues that escalated the confrontation and diminished the constructive problem-solving space to one solution, would you really want to spray peaceful demonstrators who are your own students? When you see yourself on film, do you want to be remembered as a person who injures the harmless? Of course, the behavior is easy to dismiss by saying, "I was just following orders." "I don't make the laws; I just enforce them." (How many times have we had to listen to that in history?)

One of our fathers was a career police officer in the metropolitan Cleveland area: a tattoo-layered former navy tough guy with no sympathy for bad people. But he would not have pepper-sprayed students on a college campus, nor would he have given orders to do so. In deciding what to do, you have to weigh not only what is legal against what is illegal, but what is moral against what is immoral. Admittedly, these are hard trade-offs to make, but a good leader gets you to think about both sides of the equation before you act; at least that allows a broader range of options to be entertained. In contrast, poor leaders depend on stooges to rotely carry out their dirty work. All kinds of actions are technically justifiable. The day, however, will pass, and on the next day you will want to know that the people who work for you will do their jobs well *and* with honor.

There is a scene in the movie *Saving Private Ryan* when the Americans overcome a German position, suffering casualties as a consequence. One unarmed German soldier remains, and there are two options available, accompanied by strident discussion. The character played by Tom Hanks, the squad's commander, muses about how he wants to think of himself when the war is over and leaves it to his men to decide the fate of the German. They release him. There are two items of note from this brief scene. First, the commander was able to get his troops to reflect on their potential actions and what they might personally imply. Second, he allowed them to make the choice. Had he dictated the solution one way or another, the men in his care would never have learned anything, since they would have been "just following orders."

A recent book, aptly titled *Beautiful Souls*, talks about the courageous acts of ordinary, unassuming people.[3] These are people who, despite the possibility of significant repercussions for disobeying orders, did the right thing, mostly by saving lives and relieving the suffering of others. We encounter choices all the time. We often see the tragic results of those choices when things go terribly wrong, as when a preventable disaster, such as an oil rig exploding and collapsing in the Gulf of Mexico, occurs. No matter what the ultimate consequences are, people always are responsible for their own actions. But a great deal of blame for disastrous outcomes can be assigned to leaders who no longer seem to know what the right thing is and, therefore, are impotent in positively affecting the behavior of others.

## Community

There is a positive connotation to the fountains we mentioned previously that we want to return to. Fountains are often works of art, but they are places where people congregate, too. Art cultivates exchange, social cohesion, and intimacy. In some sense, museums do us a disservice because they foster a sense of estrangement and solitude—and annoyance when people stand in your way. We, on the other hand, think of art as a social activity where people are keen to find common ground and a close connection to one another. In fact, some of the works we enjoy are those of Barnett Newman, whose horizontally elongated sweeps of color evoke communal movement: we sense others beside us, moving in concert with us as we edge along the piece.

Pieces of art like Bernini's work in the piazza inspire assembly, forging connections among members of a community, friends and strangers alike. A leader's job is similar to that of a glorious fountain in a busy mall: to bring people productively and harmoniously together in a way that is exciting and fulfilling, often in a manner in which the leader's (artist's) presence is felt but not seen. One way to do this within a corporation, of course, is to orchestrate group events. But that is the lesser option and one that frequently appears contrived. A more promising and difficult alternative is to preserve the artistry in people so that they willingly seek out new experiences, appreciate beauty, remain enterprising, enjoy the work of others, and are open to collaborations. The old-fashioned and understated description may be to maintain morale. We think a leader is much more important than that. Leaders with generative, spirited, and team-centric people in their organizations have found ways to keep the work significant and their people's psyches intact.

# Chapter 11

# Context: Right Time, Place, and Methods

**Question: Do I manifest a distinctive management style, and am I able to adapt my style and approach in order to fit the conditions in which I am operating?**

*Mother, no, do not cry,*
*Queen of heaven most chaste*
*Help me always.*
*Hail Mary.*

"Helena Wanda Blazusiakówna" from
*Third Symphony*, Henryk Górecki

A recurring question in the arts is whether nonaesthetic properties—those things outside the object—have any bearing on our attitudes toward the object itself. For example, would knowing that the quote provided at the start of the chapter from Górecki's chillingly beautiful *Third Symphony*, or *Symphony of Sorrowful Songs*, was lifted off the wall of a Gestapo prison make a difference in your assessment of the work? Would knowing that it was written by a selfless 18-year-old girl who was more concerned for her mother than her own horrifying situation alter the way you hear the music (the girl survived the war)? Many people who perennially put Górecki's work on the British and American pop charts were unlikely to be aware of its theme of mortality and redemption and of unwavering love between parent and child. The context of the three-part lament is wartime Poland, where, in addition to 3 million Jews, an equivalent number of Poles lost their lives (including several from Górecki's family). Clearly the lyrically soothing tune is no lullaby. It is a piece filled with hope amid horror, never sinking to gratuitous sentimentalism, but instead offering a transcendent journey through unthinkable brutality. The *Third Symphony* is already one of the best-selling classical recordings of all time. If more people were aware of the origins of its passion, we suspect even more downloads of this great work would follow.

To write such a magnificent work, Górecki followed a general set of technical and compositional rules that not only positioned the piece historically but also provided the composer with the means of creation. Those who have become numbed by bizarre works of art involving bodily fluids, fire bricks, and rotting foods, and who have come to believe that anything can pass as art, have lost sight of the fact that most art, no matter how foreign its material components may seem, is built upon traditions and transitions from them.

Górecki abandoned his original predilection for the serialist 12-tone compositional technique of Schoenberg and others for another technical form: minimalism. As it happens, minimalism has a history with unique period sounds that range from early chants, to Pachelbel's *Canon in D Major*, to Satie's *3 Gymnopédies*, to Ravel's *Bolero*, to our present time. As the term implies, *minimalist music* contains few notes, few words, few instruments, reiteration of musical phrases, repetition and a steady pulse, and soft versus jarring dissonance. Philip Glass may be the best known of the modern minimalist composers, but we believe Morton Lauridsen's inspiring tonal choral works would qualify as well.

Our point is that Górecki wasn't making up the rules, but was following a lengthy tradition. He was giving a contemporary edge to a style of music that has been around for centuries. Working within the minimalist tradition, Górecki had written a work that appeals to twenty-first-century sensitivities. Indeed, one of the things that makes this work, art, is that it conforms to a class of objects that we already have accepted as art.

The fact that art builds on tradition has two consequences. One is that it allows us to accept objects that would have been gut wrenching to audiences of prior generations. Imagine unveiling a painting of Campbell's Soup cans or performing rap to the aristocracy of eighteenth-century France. Second, it allows us to reinterpret: Rubens's nonidealized figures that departed from classical treatment were considered unbecoming in his time but are perfectly tame today when contrasted with Renoir's work. Common threads that run through art history mean that our interpretations of art may change with context and time, and we can change our minds in either direction, from past to present and present to past. Likewise, progressions in art can render some works dated, while other artists, who were ahead of their time (van Gogh and Modigliani, for example), gain currency.

Artists develop styles for which they are known. That is, artists have selective preferences regarding the perceptual elements that give their work an identifiable individuality. If you listen to Górecki regularly and look at enough of Modigliani's work, you will come to appreciate how they see the world through the distinctive and recognizable means in which they reveal it. Style, which comes from the Latin *stilus*, a pointed writing instrument, gives an artwork a referential character, a signature that identifies the artist and, as important, heightens our interest in the artist and his or her work.

---

## A Common Language

Leadership exists within the context of a broader business milieu that has an established set of rules and practices and a specific language associated with it. There are accepted ways to think about the financial and nonfinancial aspects of business and the ways in which organizations are structured and operate. The value of this common understanding becomes apparent whenever such understandings are absent. We typically see this when working with nonprofit institutions in which the leadership team frequently has very little formal business training. Communications are very difficult since the language that we take for granted seems foreign in some organizations without strong business orientations. A part of the work becomes providing a vocabulary about common methods, practices, and processes in order to facilitate ongoing dialogue.

In addition to needing a common frame of reference to talk about options and actions, organizations use different templates for capital and authority structures that not only give these organizations different feels, but also dictate in large measure how things are done. Stock companies operate differently from partnerships, and centralized and hierarchical organizations work differently from organizations in which there is greater diffusion of accountability. Leadership, then, doesn't float around in a vacuum. Leadership operates in a context and has to be understood and evaluated within those parameters. The context includes not only historical precedents, but situational variables such as the organization's culture and design. The context will affect how the leader executes certain tasks, but he or she always retains the ability to make modifications, just as Górecki altered his organizing principles and method of creating music. We can imagine that Górecki made the switch from serialism to minimalism because a song of prayer calls for a composition that is solemn, comforting, simple, and ennobling. Therefore, a principal task for a leader is deciding whether his or her goals and approach are appropriate for the context. Do the ideas a leader wishes to express fit with situational requirements and his or her stylistic inclinations? Regardless of the choice, there has to be a rational coherence in which to act. Leadership is necessarily lodged within a meaningful system that contains inputs, throughputs, and outputs.

## Evolving Tastes and Conditions

Tastes and conditions change. Art moves forward, and what is contextually understandable in one era may be incomprehensible in another. In addition, because of cultural differences, works that are clear to one cultural group may be confusing to another. Therefore, what appears wrongheaded at one place or time seems prescient in other locales and decades, and vice versa.

This historical and cultural transience creates a bit of a moving target when it comes to evaluating leadership. Fluctuating external business conditions, new internal organizational structures due to factors such as mergers and acquisitions, the passage of time and shifts in popular attitudes, and growing cultural diversity all may collectively affect leadership. In turn, these factors either may expose a leader's ability to adapt or may reveal serious flaws when faced with new operating conditions and circumstances. Given this, we often want to see how a leader performs over a prolonged period of time before rendering a final opinion of his or her abilities, if the results of a leader's effectiveness aren't strikingly evident sooner. Changes due to time, place, or audience may compel us to qualify our evaluation of a leader by concluding that he or she demonstrated superb leadership skills within one context but wasn't as successful in another. The most evident example is a leader who flourishes in start-ups but who struggles in larger, more mature institutions.

Providing qualifying statements makes more sense than judging a particular leader to be both good and bad. Think of how foolish it would sound if we were to change our minds about the value of a work of art on an annual basis, vacillating back and forth between positive and negative assessments. In general, the better a leader is able to bridge boundaries erected by time and circumstance, the more enduring his or her leadership and the larger the size of the audience will tend to be.

Most often you have to wait and see how works are embraced over time as new evidence and awareness accumulate. This allows prior shortcomings or failures to catch up with executives who are serial movers: those who have an uncanny ability to look good in the short-term, but move on to a new employer before things at their old institution go south and the leaders' drawbacks come into sharper focus. Good leadership, then, presupposes a healthy understanding of history about where things have been and where they are heading, with the more informed students of the past and the more intuitive students of the future having a better chance of success.

Thankfully for us, one (or two or three) errant tries do not a failure make if one understands the history, context, and direction of a business. We're thinking of the late Steve Jobs, who had his fair share of duds such as the Apple III, the Lisa PC, the early Macintosh, and NeXT. But from these "failures," elegant designs, the first graphical interfaces, and progressive software emerged. Collectively, Steve Jobs's future legendary market successes were made possible by his early forays into technology and by what he learned along the way. There came a time when the right ingredients and execution converged, and the public applauded.

## Style

A part of our understanding and appreciation of others comes from the characteristic ways in which they behave, quirks and all. Over time, leaders develop distinctive ways of doing and relating. Perceived departures from customary modes of behavior are described as "not his style." Great artists are known for a style that is representative of their temperaments and personalities, which are embedded in their works. Minor figures emulate the style of others. The same can be said for greater or lesser leaders, but we add an important qualifier: great artists also know the conditions under which their style will work. Many of their experimental attempts to apply their techniques to subjects that aren't accepting of them end up in the trash bin.

The idea of style is easy to understand if you walk into the different work spaces and offices of your colleagues. You will find that your associates have selected different ways to arrange elements within their perceptual field, with some people working in the sloppy style (stacks and more stacks), the picturesque style (photos and placards galore), or the spare style (does anybody work here?). Within each of these styles, the individual may stand out. There are many ways to be sloppy, after all. An inventive slob may punch holes in the corners of papers and hang them from fish hooks that are attached to the ceiling, creating floating stacks. Thus, working within the sloppy tradition, your colleague may produce a signature style based on his or her personal attitudes, traits, values, motives, etc. There will be no other sloppy office just like it.

In leadership, there are too many individualistic styles to classify, but you can think about your general approach and ask whether it would be as effective with a different employee group or under more or less stressful economic conditions. Would you be able to lead as effectively if there were notable performance problems in the group? How would you fare in a different division with a different functional focus or in a different industry, as James McNerney, Jr., for example, has done in moving from GE to 3M to Boeing? We have seen leaders thrive when using what may be described as a laissez-faire style (little focus provided, for example, instilling a "figure it out for yourself" climate) with highly educated and trained professional staffs, but flounder under other circumstances where a more directive style may have been necessary. Leaders, in this case, will need either to adapt their style or to stick to the materials, setting, and conditions where their work will more likely succeed. Artists tend to choose the latter. In electing the former, leaders may have to become proficient in criteria that they possess in nominal quantities. They will have to become better at what they had heretofore not needed to master.

This does not imply that leaders need to take an elixir in order to transform themselves back and forth between Jekyll and Hyde. You don't have to change your personality or your belief system in order to recognize that circumstances may call for a different behavioral press from what you are most accustomed to and comfortable with. You want to find ways to play to your strengths, but you need to recognize that those strengths, under certain conditions, may become liabilities unless you are able to make adjustments. For example, being more directive when people are uncertain concerning what to do, or are unaware of what a project outcome should look like, doesn't mean that you have momentarily assumed an authoritarian personality. In fact, it means you are willing to help someone who doesn't know how to proceed, which may require more straightforward instructions; but it doesn't change who you are as a person. This may be exceptionally hard for some people to do since they may not enjoy giving direct orders and loathe being confrontational. Ultimately, however, people want to know that regardless of the specific decisions you make, you remain essentially unchanged and true to your values. And being flexible is not the same as being disingenuous.

# Chapter 12

# Criticism: Take Me Seriously, Please

**Question: Am I worthy of being judged and appreciated as a leader?**

Poster from the film *Maniac*
(Magnum Motion Pictures, Inc., 1980)

The late film critic Gene Siskel admittedly walked out of three films. The illustrated poster, on the facing page, depicts one of them: *Maniac*. *Maniac* is a highly graphic splatter film in which a potbellied wacko randomly kills and scalps women, dressing up mannequins in his apartment with their clothing and remains. The scant plot is simply a vehicle to introduce serial violence.

By criticism we don't intend to engage in the contested question of "Who is to judge?" We are content to maintain that a judge of taste is a person who has substantial experience in the subject matter and is capable of directing us to objects that will yield satisfying experiences . . . and leave it at that. Hume, Kant, and others would all agree that a critic is a person who knows what he or she is talking about. However, like Siskel, we believe that not everything presented as art can be evaluated as art because, let's say, the creator doesn't have the talent, hasn't tried hard enough, or has other purposes in mind. The "artist's" aim wasn't to produce anything of reasonable complexity or depth, but to manipulate us or amuse us, or in the case of *Maniac*, gross us out. Despite looking at the work through a special lens that art invites, we are unable to see anything of redeeming value and can only conclude that further attention would be a waste of our time. It isn't art, doesn't try to be art, will never be art. These hopeless cases should come with a warning label: "Although what you are viewing, heuristically, may be referred to as art, any value you derive from your observations will be purely accidental." Therefore, in order to qualify as art, the work must be able to meet a minimum threshold of artistic value.

More critically problematic instances of art arise when the art itself is good but remains difficult to appreciate. The prototypical example is Leni Riefenstahl's film *Triumph of Will*, in which she enthusiastically (and unapologetically) portrays the 1934

Nazi Party rally. We could have easily used a frame from this film's footage as our prime example for this chapter. The film's distinguishing quality is that in spite of its advocacy of Hitler's cause, it transformed the way documentaries are made. The innovative camera work and film angles convey intense energy and excitement. In addition, Riefenstahl departed from the usual chronological sequence of documentary filmmaking, choosing to film out of order but to cut and paste in a manner that gave the film a sense of order and unity—albeit a thematic integration based on a celebration of hatred. Technically speaking, this is a finely made film.

The issue with the film is that its message is so morally repugnant that it is difficult to acknowledge the craft behind it. The expertly made propaganda is too vile and contrary to normal human sentiments to recognize the artistry or to view the film as a work of art. The work counts as an artistic failure because these underpinnings make it impossible to respond to art in the way the artist prescribes. Expressions of ethically abhorrent attitudes surely must be included as artistic defects. Great art can be ugly: Matisse referred to Picasso's *Les Demoiselles* as "the hideous whores of Avignon." It can be gnawingly raw, like Bartók's *Miraculous Mandarin*. And it can be disturbing, as in Picasso's great antiwar painting, *Guernica*. But *Guernica* depicts the horrors of war (the Spanish Civil War) and the suffering it inflicts on innocents; it does not celebrate warmongering and ethnic cleansing.

An important part of art appreciation is being prepared to take a work seriously: to make some effort to discover what it is all about and to take in what it has to offer. That is, it is worthy of criticism because there is the presumption of some value. But when the encounter is explicitly repulsive or cheap, then the best course may be the one taken by Siskel: to walk out.

# Not Everyone Can Be Called a Leader

A primary aim of the leader is to make others successful and to achieve results that the organization requires for its continuation. However, when leaders only create interpersonal problems where they did not exist, obstruct progress, repeatedly demonstrate little tact by breaking confidences and verbally brutalizing others, then they neither should be taken seriously nor be held up as leaders. Indeed, such leaders should have their stripes ceremoniously ripped off. They should, at a minimum, be demoted or, more appropriately, terminated.

We use the term *leader* too loosely in organizations. Companies can't afford to tolerate the inane and ridiculous as if the position itself confers leadership and entitles the incumbent to automatic regard. Not everything hung on a wall or shown in a theater counts as art. It is an unfortunate part of organizational life that somehow people devoid of all skill and respect for others obtain positions of authority. Indeed, some excellent leaders we know should be outraged by a brand of leadership that groups them with "leaders" who are undeserving of the name. Not everyone in a position of authority is worth taking seriously: there are those who have too many flaws, are too vile, and have nothing of significance to offer. In the words of many of the employees with whom we have spoken, these people are a joke, and the companies to which these people belong fail to see that they just aren't funny—they are destructive. People who can't manage others, shouldn't, as they are missing the essential building blocks of excellence in leadership—such human traits as compassion, integrity, and gratitude.

## Values Count

Let's be blunt. It is hard to follow someone who espouses values contrary to what we know to be right and good. The Riefenstahl documentary may well have opened a new era of documentary filmmaking, but her art will always remain associated with its message rather than its method. It wasn't a satirical or subtle attempt to expose a corrupt regime but a genuine effort to glorify a cause that all but the thoroughly brainwashed and willfully blind opposed. People do follow the wrong path and are persuaded or coerced into believing that their actions are proper, but the leader who instigates such actions is no good, and there is no history that will redeem his or her reputation.

Often the cases you will experience aren't as severe as the Riefenstahl case, but issues of character and credibility do repeatedly arise—and worse, they will arise with your closest friends, and you will have a decision to make. Suppose a close friend of yours is discovered to have been viewing pornographic materials in his office by his direct reports. What do you do? Do you explain it away as a boyish prank, or do you ask for his resignation? President Clinton kept his job following his proven dalliance inside the Oval Office, but his credibility was shot, and his term was thereafter crippled. The reason that character counts is because credibility counts. It is critical for people to believe that the person who controls their fates and with whom they have freely aligned themselves will act with proper conviction and in a manner that reflects their personal values.

## Effective Does Not Mean Good

We are repeatedly struck by the tolerance of many companies toward people who are highly compromised. Most often, these are people who make money while simultaneously doing immeasurable damage to morale and to the organization. Organizational success is predicated on teamwork, and no one, no matter how good he or she is, should stand taller than the team. Good leaders worry about the welfare of the group first and foremost.

Riefenstahl was one of the towering figures of documentary film-making at the time, but is this the sort of person you would want affiliated with your interests?

In our consulting, we have listened to tortured executives weigh the psychological immaturity (which is a euphemism for "nutty behavior") of their highest producers against the kind of company they would ideally want. Their ponderous deliberations never last long since money usually wins out. We sometimes believe that these "tough" decisions arise for our benefit as a sort of secret code that at once communicates the true values the speaker harbors and the difficulty of his or her job. It says neither to us since the campaign to keep a productive scourge runs afoul of what we believe is true. It has never been hard for us to fire high-performing lone wolves if they couldn't abide by norms of decency. Why? We have never seen a group perform worse when the best but most egotistical performer has been let go. In fact, the typical consequence is that everyone else does better following the departure of subversive types. Disagreement is fine. Having to deal daily with disagreeable people is not.

## Many Ways to Make a Point

We are not arguing for universal niceties: life isn't always pleasant. We are arguing for universal civility and respect. As the examples embedded in our illustrative discourse make clear, realities can be harsh or even ugly. And there is nothing wrong with making a point by depicting the opposite. The Spanish Civil War was brutal, and Picasso depicted it like that in order to reveal its underbelly, not for each side to fight harder and more defiantly. There are many ways to be serious and to be taken seriously—which, by the way, doesn't eliminate humor as a legitimate means to make a point. Overall, however, in order to be taken seriously, your interest in your people must be unwavering, the pursuit of your intentions resolute, and the ways that you capture people's attention both manifold and substantive.

Superfluous leaders think they have a job, as opposed to a responsibility. They don't care what their employees think or how others are affected by the decisions they make; they lose sight of their goals and aimlessly flounder; they don't know how to make a point worth listening to or remembering. They have a penchant for making off-center remarks and engaging in offensive behavior. They don't know of what their art consists and, without a rudimentary understanding of their real work, they have no way of figuring it out. Leadership is lost on them because they wouldn't know where to begin. They speak a language unknown to those who are true practitioners of the art of leadership. They are unknowingly or indifferently ineffective, and while that can make them unstable and unpredictable, it also makes them a liability to the success of the company.

# Chapter 13

# Do We Really Not Care About Leadership?

We have done a fair amount of consulting with companies in the area of compensation. One of the things that executives hate most in this arena is incentive plans that pay out for qualitative results when there isn't sufficient funding—basically having to pay for something that isn't affordable. We understand this opposition and agree. In response, however, some companies have thrown out the proverbial baby with the bathwater and have rejected the use of qualitative metrics altogether in sole favor of monetary measurements. That, in turn, creates the problem that *we* hate: paying executives for long-term performance, as almost always measured by stock price, when there has been no noticeable short-term improvement in the company's operations as qualitative improvements would have indicated. If the company hasn't proved itself to be more efficient, timely, and responsive to customers, innovative in product development and distribution, and so on, then why pay for a higher stock price, a measure that can be manipulated and timed? Indeed, the stock price almost always is used as a proxy for leadership prowess, which is a flawed measure on many counts.

To begin with, we want to briefly explore a false equation: the purported equivalency between results and leadership. The result we are speaking about is the most common one of returns on shareholder investment as delivered through the price of company stock. Suppose a company's share price does substantially increase. Does that in itself give us reason to admire a leader's achievement? We know that plenty of people will relish the results, but will they have reason to appreciate the leader for what he or she has done in increasing shareholder wealth? Thankfulness is far from appreciation of skill and accomplishment.

We think there are several reasons to be suspicious of the exclusive use of financial results (we use stock price as our target, but what we say applies to most of the usual financial outcome measures) as a proxy for leadership. First, there are broad economic factors that affect stock price, enabling CEOs to ride surges in business to stardom. Second, stock price may be influenced by world events that, say, heighten the need for certain commodities, bolstering prices and stock performances within certain industries, accordingly. Third, as we now know all too well, companies can affect the number of outstanding shares and massage earnings in order to influence the price of stock. Therefore, it is possible to stretch accounting standards and financial maneuvers to their creative limits and paint a flattering portrait of corporate prosperity that is exaggerated.

We are not questioning the importance of results—we want to be clear about that. Instead, we want to point out two drawbacks with overreliance on end results:

1. Even if the problems noted above did not exist, the outcome measures most frequently used as indexes of corporate success still are not true indicators of accomplishment.

2. An overemphasis on results can counterproductively
   lead to an underemphasis of process and leadership.

In the following paragraphs, we address each of these in turn.

We don't believe that anyone would disagree that companies
are engaged in a fierce worldwide competition, which seems to be
getting tougher daily. Most countries have laws that try to assure
that a competitive market environment is maintained, domesti-
cally and internationally. Although it is politically fashionable to
single out a few international punching bags such as China, for
the most part attempts are made to assure global equity in trade.
As a competition, there are winners and losers, but we have a
system where anyone "can step right up" because "everyone is a
winner." If the stock goes up and vests within a prescribed time,
you win no matter how other companies may have performed.

Under no circumstance would we pay for performances that
were not indicative of true achievement: that there was reasonable assurance that what was done within the company led to
results that, when compared with a composite scale of competitors' performances, demonstrated genuine success. To use a
sports analogy, currently boards and consultants are prepared to
reward handsomely and to admire those leaders whose companies have recorded the equivalent of their fastest times (had good
results irrespective of how others have performed). However,
we don't place laurels on people who have run their fastest in
the Olympics; we recognize the people who cross the finish line
first, second, and third. The gold medal goes to the winner, not
to the person who has attained his or her personal best time.
Therefore, our first point is that results are indeed important but
only if it is possible to ascribe some measure of achievement to
the outcomes.

Let's now continue with the second point. It may be possible to limit how much acclaim we affix to a leader, even if the

company generates exalted results that were fairly measured. Even the best of legitimately obtained results cannot be used reliably to judge the quality of leadership unless certain conditions exist. Preliminarily, it is easy to conceive instances in which a company achieves great results but has lousy leadership. The company may have been in the right place at the right time with the right idea (been extremely lucky); traded a secure future for pleasing intermediate earnings (will exercise the "long-gone" tactic—by the time the trade-off is discovered, the leader will be long gone); unexpectedly benefited from the miscues of chief competitors (weren't particularly smart, just less stupid); obtained a near-monopoly position through aggressive lobbying (kept real competitors off the playing field); and so forth. Results are due to many factors unrelated to leadership. It is possible to win, but to win ugly.

Our fear is that if the ends become integral to one's thinking about leadership, then process progressively loses its relevance and perceived importance. The quality of leadership becomes an afterthought. If a sprinter is first to break the tape, a swimmer is first to touch the wall, or a football team accumulates more points during the course of play, they all win. We might revel in an elegant stride, beautiful stroke, or acrobatic catch, but the mode of victory is irrelevant when the ends are clear and the supreme goal is winning. We will quickly forgive the unorthodox style of a runner, unusual stroke of a free stylist, or lucky catch of a receiver, if the individuals and team all win. Similarly, we don't deduct points for bad form in these events, because as long as play remains within the rules, the only thing that matters, as the late great coach of the Green Bay Packers Vince Lombardi once said, is winning. We really don't care how a team wins, just as long as it wins.

When corporate emphasis shifts toward results—and often these are short-term results—we run the risk of demoting leadership in importance because the market doesn't care how you got your results as long as they were obtained legally; and even here it seems the markets allow plenty of wiggle room. It is possible to be a good businessperson, excellent financier, and marvelous deal maker but still not be a very a good leader. The knack these individuals have is for making money; certainly moneymaking skills are not bad skills to have, but they're not the same ones required for leadership. It is a facile connection to make and one that sells magazines, but leadership and results are not the same. In essence, when we begin to attend exclusively to outcomes, we start to lose sight of all the things that are under a company's control and that can contribute to the results. For example, we forget the fact that leadership really does matter and can make a profound difference in how your company performs over an extended period of time.

Do sales determine the greatness of art? Do we measure artistic value by consumers' response to it? To be sure, we tend to pay much more for great art, but that is because we have already determined it was great. Artistic merit preceded the price tag. More often than not, we would expect good leaders to outcompete their rivals and essentially have something tangible to show for their efforts. But we wouldn't appreciate them as leaders unless they did something identifiable that makes them and their work worthy of our admiration. This brings us back to the subject of this book and the sorts of things we would look for in a leader-artist. The list we have produced is comprehensive, but you need not excel at every criterion named to be considered good. Nevertheless, there has to be something of perceptible value behind the orchestration of the company's activities and one's relationship to the employee population, which demands respect for the skill involved. That is, there has to be some evidence that the results were achieved in a way in which we can attribute genuine accomplishment to the leader. This differentiates the relentless cost cutter whose exploits over a three-year span dramatically increase earnings from a person who prudently and artistically reshapes a company while minimizing the detrimental effects on the company's future prospects—and makes money doing it. The former person creates a wasteland bereft of focused, forward energy and employee engagement. The second person, a leader, shepherds people through the trials of a troubled company while enlarging their interests and capacities to perform en route. The leader makes financial progress and, at the same time, preserves the company's ability to produce and compete over the long run.

There are caveats to what we just said. Although we would expect a leader to obtain healthy results over a reasonable period, for example, there may be exceptions. First, like artists who toil and pass in obscurity—later to be posthumously discovered—results do not always tell the whole story. A person may have done all the right things a leader should do without getting the results sought or the attention deserved because the market may not have been prepared for the offering. A foundation was in place, but it took time for the ideas to percolate before being embraced by an enthusiastic public. It is unfortunate, but sometimes great works sit unnoticed until someone, in retrospect, notes, "He was right all along." For example, although Robert Nardelli was a cultural mismatch for Home Depot with regard to his leadership style, which was more rigid than the entrepreneurial company could stomach, we don't believe he has received enough credit for streamlining operations and improving the supply chain. He was very strong on maintaining organizational *focus*, and he created a new, integrated *form* among people, processes, and technology that increased efficiency. These alone don't necessarily grant the status of greatness. Rather, we suggest that, in retrospect, there are elements of his tenure as CEO that succeeded but that are blurred by failures in other areas, such as *context*—not paying enough attention to the corporate history, customs, and institutional norms.

Second, a leader who keeps a company from failing may not be popularly hailed a success, but keeping a company alive and out of bankruptcy may be seen as a leadership triumph. Similarly, a leader who eschews higher quarterly earnings in order to reposition the company to a changing marketplace will not become a darling of Wall Street but may become a savior to a future generation of workers. For example, when companies elect to increase investments in research and development, you can hear the moans from Wall Street. It is easy to produce the names of companies that appeased analysts for too long and failed to act decisively sooner: Kodak for one. Steve Sasson is credited with the invention of the first digital camera at Kodak in 1975, and Kodak produced what we believe was the first megapixel camera. Yet, today, the company is in bankruptcy, and its camera business has been closed. For two kids—the authors—who grew up in northeastern Ohio and who considered the not-too-distant Rochester, New York, an Emerald City of corporate America, the company's decline is sad indeed.

# Chapter 14

# Masters of Leadership

Perhaps it is best to begin a chapter on pedagogy with a simple fact. Some of the greatest artists and businesspeople had little formal education. Certainly Rembrandt never received a diploma for a master's in fine arts, nor did artists such as Picasso or de Kooning. Jackson Pollock never finished high school. Cornelius Vanderbilt left school at age 11; Henry Ford left the family farm at 17 to become an apprentice machinist in Detroit; and as everyone knows, tech titans Bill Gates and Larry Ellison never finished college. Nevertheless, today both the MFA and MBA are ubiquitous degrees and nearly essential credentials in the arts and business, respectively. Recruiters eagerly look for the abbreviations on résumés. Galleries and corporations often require them. The better the school, the bigger the initials appear to the naked eye. Those letters, write large in caps, create instantaneous creditability and the all-important network for entry into the most prestigious companies and showplaces.

Cherry-picked cases do not constitute an argument for or against advanced formal training in the arts or business. We could have easily presented countercases. John D. Rockefeller was an educated man of his day, and many current CEOs have advanced degrees: over 150 CEOs in the Fortune 500 have MBAs; and the largest company by revenues, Walmart, is headed by Mike Duke, who has a bachelor of science degree in industrial engineering from the Georgia Institute of Technology. Eric Schmidt, the former CEO of Google, has a BS in electrical engineering from Princeton and a PhD in electrical engineering and computer science from the University of California, Berkeley. Also, in just a span of a few years during the 1960s, the Yale School of Fine Arts produced the likes of Richard Serra, Fred Sandback, Nancy Graves, and Brice Marden.

Although not an argument, the examples and counter-examples produce questions about what a student of any age gets beyond his or her undergraduate training by enrolling in advanced programs that are intended to produce ... ahh, hmm. We suppose that introduces our first issue. Let's stick to business for the moment and ask the basic question of what an MBA is intended to do. It isn't necessary to provide an expansive critique, since there have been sufficient numbers of intelligent reviews of the traditional MBA degree from highly regarded scholars such as Henry Mintzberg and Warren Bennis, who have derided the degree as being big on numbers and woefully short on other forms of knowledge that are messier and not as easy to quantify.[1] Those fields have been plowed before. In fact, a simple article search shows that the MBA has been under attack for at least 50 years. Our aim is to keep the tone of our criticisms friendly and focused in order to improve leadership training within the context of the MBA, and not to launch an all-out assault. We want to move on, constructively, from where we are to what we envision as more fertile ground.

It would be laughable if a business program were to seriously claim that it is "turning out leaders of the future." Rather, these programs turn out people who will become senior executives and who, mostly, will make quite a bit of money—but we would be hard-pressed to see how the programs turn out leaders. In many graduate-level business curricula, students are able to pass through the two-year program without having to ever take a class in leadership, not that it would do much good anyway. Leadership often is taught as the acquisition of a set of skills that supposedly are scientifically determinable, as if a leader's actions could be reduced to a set of if-then clauses—we know that doesn't work. There are too many intangibles that simply cannot be taught using conventional classroom methods. As is clear from everything we say in this book, we view leadership as an art, as a lifelong endeavor. It involves an ongoing process of refinement and thickening of skin—the ability to take criticism that comes very close to being personal and use it to one's benefit. It involves the mastery of motivation, recognition of complex relations, creativity (mixed in with a dose of courage), and a deep concern for people. And, yet, what we often get instead by the admission of the ultimate insiders, the deans of prominent business schools, are management models devoid of a human presence.[2]

We both have been parts of MBA programs, and we appreciate the dedication of the full-time faculty. But if you look at what is being taught, it is mostly hard skills, with accounting and finance leading the way. Why? Those are the quantitatively oriented areas with zip lines to Wall Street, private equity companies, and hedge funds. If MBA programs were honest with themselves, they would readily admit—and some do—that they are preparing students to fill important corporate skill-based roles that (and this is mostly unsaid) would give them an equitable return on their sizable educational investment. A program that emphasized soft skills or leadership would see its admissions and rankings dwindle to a trickle unless the cost of admission similarly declined. In fairness, some programs, to prove their growing commitment to the more intangible elements of leadership, have added electives, mainly in the areas of critical, analytical, and design thinking—a grudging and nominal display of open-mindedness.

One way to think of this state of affairs is in terms of a hopelessly cyclical trap. Deviate from the science-based skills model that plants people through networks (and genuine expertise) into lucrative positions, and the school will lose the big donations, fancy buildings, elevated faculty salaries, high rankings, and, ultimately, the students. We suppose that schools could justify the current model by maintaining that it is preparatory and not final—that the true intent is to expose students to a broad range of subjects that they later can hone through their corporate experiences. That may be true, but we still believe that the MBA has plenty of room for improvement. Anyway, why allow our corporations to become the finishing schools for the MBA at the prices that students are paying?

Our feeling is that business schools are moving in the wrong direction if they truly want to produce leaders. Schools are conceiving imaginative ways to shorten the learning period, whereas we think it should be lengthened to include instruction directly concerned with leadership if these schools want to reduce the frequency with which the technocrats they produce turn into autocrats and, then, into monsters. An MBA program would never pass a student who repeatedly fails accounting and finance. We wouldn't want to see that student pass either, because mastery of these subjects is fundamental to the proper exercise of business. But isn't leadership? Would you pass someone whose leadership style was hopelessly flawed?

We very recently encountered a situation in which human resources was teaching a manager to be more humane. Trying to teach humanity to humans is a little like trying to teach Godzilla to be less clumsy or Lex Luther to be less sinister. A specimen of an accelerated MBA program, he now wreaks havoc on those without the benefit of a similar instructional background—but who know all too well what that education has yielded.

We tend to think of the MBA as a significant opportunity for students, but we believe too little is taught in too little time. And we believe there is unevenness in instruction in which learning is geared to the cerebral centers of the brain that hit analytics but that miss the emotional areas fundamental to understanding what makes people tick and how work actually gets done and why. At the very least, business schools could make the word *emotion* less frightening for graduates in order for them to go out into the world and feel at ease in using it in conversation. Today, we know executives who reject the idea of emotional intelligence simply because it sounds too mushy and unbusinesslike. A great deal of business is all about emotion, and yet it is quarantined as if it were a pox. We are afraid that a clinical sterility has crept into the curriculum and is producing highly analytical people who are detached from common sense, moral fortitude, and life-affirming values.

We will always recall the executive who attended one of the grand liberal arts institutions in the United States and then obtained his MBA. Let's just say, in the words of the Decemberists ("Shankill Butchers" from *The Crane Wife*), "that something went horribly askew." He was one of the most illiberal, hard-hearted men we ever met. He was unable to control insensitive and unnecessary outbursts and lacked awareness of proper versus improper, right versus wrong. We felt like taking him by the ear and returning him to his undergraduate and graduate institutions and telling them to fix him. Indeed, some MBA programs are offering remedial ethics courses free of charge to graduates, but in reality, we don't believe it will do much good. It is hard to undo one's moral upbringing. It is easier to teach people how to confront ethical digressions in the workplace constructively, as Mary Gentile has ably done in the progressive program described in her book *Giving Voice to Values*.[3]

If there is a general trend across business schools, it is to get as many students through the program as quickly as possible at increasing prices. If MBA programs produce leaders, they do so only in the students' own minds—in the mistaken belief that the degree, coupled with specialized expertise and authority over a group, equals leadership. MBA programs owe the business community much more than that, especially given that corporations frequently pay the way for their employees. We would expect that these companies would insist on more in return.

Technical proficiency is important. The world is bigger than ever, production chains are more complex, corporations are increasingly large and sophisticated, and advanced technical skills are necessary and require extended training times to perfect. There is a need, but the need is much larger than currently embraced and incompletely satisfied by two years of coursework, a couple of summer internships, case-study analyses, and a few weeks abroad. These activities will not create leaders who will be able to transform the workplace and enhance U.S. competitiveness in the world markets. Neither will graduates have the social conscience and rectitude to contain future financial debacles through a firm sense of personal responsibility and undaunted acts of selflessness. Our newfound hope in regulation will only further obscure a landscape already cluttered with trees. To find our way out of the woods, we will need a reliable compass.

Currently, the best chance of learning how to lead is to have had the benefit of good parenting and a first-company experience where leadership was seen as a specialty just like any other that cuts across an organization. The advantages of this corporate outlook are straightforward. First, companies that care about leadership watch people closely and give them timely feedback on their actions and performances, providing opportunities for up-and-coming leaders to observe and learn from more accomplished and proven leaders through mentorship programs; and using our criteria for assessment and feedback would help in the evaluation process. Second, these companies work hard to weed out leadership disasters, either channeling them in nonmanagerial directions and key sole contributor roles or pushing them out the door. Third, companies that value leadership give employees plenty of practice, trying them out on progressively difficult assignments with increasing supervisory responsibilities, offering them support and guidance as needed—and shaping their behavior, accordingly.

Now that we have expressed our cynicism of the MBA as it currently is structured, we are prepared to consider a second, related issue: how leadership might be meaningfully inserted into an MBA curriculum. What embellishments might significantly add to a student's experiences, improve corporate performance, and give greater luster to the architecturally edifying buildings of business schools? By the way, nothing might help those students who are anxious to finish the program so they can get on with their true ambition of making money, but there is always hope.

Since instructional methods tend be more delineated in the arts with two primary schools of thought, we will briefly turn our discussion back to the arts before suggesting improvements to the business curriculum. The MFA has been critiqued in much the same ways as the MBA: that it is long on technique and theory and short on the softer personalizing dimensions of practice. It provides a venue for the acquisition of specialized skills, but little that encourages significant experimentation or expands the artists' vision and unique expressions of their work. Consequently, there are debates about how best to train artists, with options taking one of two forms. On the one hand, there is today's predominately school-based system, and on the other, a studio-based system. These alternatives really provide the anchors of a continuum in which pure forms of either are improbable. Instruction tends to be a weighted blend of both: that is, the options are one of degree and emphasis versus entirely one or the other. Additionally, there are advantages and disadvantages with each approach, and therefore, we are not endorsing one over the other. With those caveats in mind, it is helpful to make the distinctions between the two pedagogical methods since our aim will be to use the distinction in explaining how business education might be enhanced.

If we may generalize, the two approaches differ to some extent on four primary dimensions:

1. The degree to which instruction is delivered by a practitioner-master

2. The degree of personalized mentorship and guidance afforded

3. The degree to which theory and the history of artistic techniques are imparted

4. The degree to which various artistic techniques are explored, practiced, and critiqued

As you might imagine, the studio is a practitioner-guided introduction into a highly specialized art practice, whereas the academic model tends to be more context-free and theory based. Obviously both share certain aspects, and when it comes to business education, our preference would be to merge the two.

In applying this model to business, it is important to see leadership as we do: as an area unto itself, like marketing or finance, that requires a defined course of study. We unequivocally reject guest speaker programs in which CEOs visit the university to speak with students *as a substitute for leadership development,* although it is a critical educational adjunct. In addition, unless a student is extremely fortunate, quality tutelage in leadership is not a necessary part of summer internships. Internships, then, are hit or miss with respect to leadership development.

It is possible to tamper more intrusively with the business model of business schools than our recommendations will do, but we would prefer to see some movement toward leadership development in our advanced degree business programs than suggest actions that would be instantly rejected (but, perhaps, we are underestimating people's motives). Overall, we don't see any way around the fact that if business instruction includes leadership as an essential construct, the time of instruction will have to somehow be lengthened. However, we think this can be achieved discreetly in a combination of four ways.

First, in addition to mandatory instruction in human behavior, students could profit from a class or two in the arts that had a business focus and was psychologically instructional to businesspeople. Not everyone would be able to tolerate the master of psychology, Shakespeare (*King Lear* and the *Henry IV and V* trilogy are popular instructional works on leadership), but a literary dose of the behaviorally astute Dickens, Melville, Austen, and James wouldn't hurt. Dickens certainly had an intimate understanding of labor, the nature of work, and bureaucracy, as *David Copperfield* and *Bleak House* can confirm. Memorable courses could easily be crafted around the visual and film arts as well. Indeed, we have been at executive retreats where senior executives have relied on snippets from films to underscore their points.

Second, it is possible to identify the artlike components of certain business courses and to teach them as art. For example, although organizational design has a few immutable principles, it is by and large a creative endeavor. When we consult on design, we warm up the group with a practice case that deals with the construction of a mythical creature. The case contains all the elements and precautions that go into reorganizations, including the effects of environmental conditions, business objectives, resource constraints, and implied assumptions on design results. The most interesting aspect of the exercise is that people can see that even though they have been provided with the exact same information, every subgroup produces a different design for its creature. We have never, in all the years we have been doing this exercise, seen the same outcome twice.

Third, we would like to see a two-year, postgraduate, practitioner-based apprenticeship in which graduates receive on-the-job coaching and periodic evaluations. This could be supplied by a third party or the company itself. The most essential element of this period is that the development of leaders be overseen by people who know what they are doing and who understand the primary material of their trade: people. It seems perfectly rational for a degree-granting institution to take some ongoing responsibility for the quality of the graduates it produces. Either that, or perhaps we should start tracking the programs that are best at fostering white-collar criminals and posting the results on the web.

Fourth, we would require graduates to attend periodic leadership retreats overseen by the business school. For example, our mutual friend Jeffrey Sonnenfeld, at the Yale University School of Management, hosts several excellent leadership programs each year, but these are directed toward current CEOs with all sorts of educational pedigrees. IESE's fine, modular Advanced Management Program has a similar focus, but as with Yale, it is open only to senior executives. Why not offer the same type of program for graduates of one's own institution? We would further suggest that these mandatory off-sites include internal reviews of the graduates. Graduates are carefully scrutinized within organizations at certain junctures in their careers, with expectations gradually rising with each cycle. The academic institution, in association with the gradu-ates' companies, could periodically take an extra-close look at its people to make sure they are capable leaders and can with-stand a public exhibition of their work.

We realize that managing paper is much easier than manag-ing people. We have mastered the former as a society and believe it is time to get on with creating real leaders of the future—in business, not-for-profits, and government. If the collective activ-ities we have specified in this chapter were adopted to some degree, business schools could express a true intent to produce well-rounded businesspeople by taking greater ongoing respon-sibility for those they send out into the business world. The quality of our institutions would assuredly benefit as a result, but as a 2012 article makes plain in describing a high-profile conflict-of-interest case involving two premier investment banks, we have a very long way to go.[4]

# The Rise and Fall of Mr. R.

The case we are about to relate is a composite of executives we have known. Our description does not reflect a single individual, but we have tried to keep our depiction consistent and familiar. While there are extreme cases on both sides of the hypothetical person we describe, we wanted to portray a person with more normative qualities, both positive and negative.

The recommended way that a company would evaluate an executive would be to gather information from multiple sources, including from people outside the company if possible. You can think of it as an enhanced 360-degree review (a review that captures information from multiple perspectives). Unfortunately, and to our great disappointment, in many instances bosses view evaluations as a duty within their sole jurisdiction and, as the putative experts, make assessments of direct reports in the absence of complete facts—and with the air that their judgment is correct and beyond dispute. We wish it weren't so, but it remains a refrain in organizations. Overly controlling executives, in particular, do not care to hear the opinions of others on matters in which they consider themselves to be experts. Even experts need the facts, and we remain steadfast supporters of 360-degree assessments. If leadership entails a close connection with followers, as most people would admit, why don't companies routinely ask the followers what they think?

We obviously believe that leadership development programs necessarily involve the perspectives of followers. First, enlisting their point of view prevents those executives who are masters of managing up from escaping the fact that their primary responsibility is to manage down. Second, including a variety of perspectives serves as a safeguard against error. In every other business activity, executives would want to act with all the available evidence on hand, but they are conspicuously less curious when it comes to people. We suspect that's because executives (like everyone else) think that they know others instinctively and that there is nothing more to learn. Psychologists, however, have repeatedly shown that individuals can be way off base in their opinions of others. The presumed trusted gut is vulnerable to bias and can be partly corrected for by the introduction of multiple points of view.

---

Mr. R. was raised in a quiet seaside town on the East Coast. He had a middle-class upbringing in a closely knit neighborhood. He attended an undistinguished college and chose to major in business administration with a specialty in accounting. He took his first job as an auditor in one of the major consultancies. His advancement at the consultancy was slow because of a lack of an advanced degree; besides, the work was extremely repetitious, and he felt it was time to move on. Therefore, after a couple of years as an auditor, he sought better opportunities elsewhere and accepted a job at a local company (Company A) in the Accounting and Finance Department.

His stay at the local institution was short-lived, lasting no more than a year. Like the consultancy, it offered little upward mobility and too much routine work. When an opportunity arose with a larger company (Company B) in a city known for its more robust business scene, he took it. Independent-minded, ambitious, and eager to show initiative, he found himself at the right place at the right time. Global markets were burgeoning; and using an old-fashioned PC, Mr. R. developed programs that would compute more precise international prices and costs, which proved to be lucrative to his host institution. That, along with other smart personal initiatives, propelled him upward and into the role of CFO within an eight-year span. He became the youngest person to ever hold that position within the company. He was not particularly liked within the department, since his meteoric rise seemed to be based primarily on one notable success that generalized to everything he touched. He could do no wrong as a favorite son of the CEO, who nurtured him along. In addition, he tended to be dismissive of the contributions of others while bathing in the glory of his success. Despite these perceptions and animosities, he was technically a capable CFO. Nevertheless, Mr. R. spent very little time supporting the development of his staff as he rose through the ranks, and in no instance during Mr. R.'s lengthy career was he ever accompanied by a staff member to a new institution when he switched companies.

Mr. R. was widely regarded as a successor to the CEO position at Company B, but a merger, which Mr. R. openly opposed for personal reasons, crushed that ambition. The new, acquiring company had its own person installed as the CEO of the joint entity. Any hope of Mr. R. reaching the top was put on hold indefinitely. Mr. R. soon thereafter sought out positions elsewhere and was hired by a larger and better-known company as its CFO (Company C). What appeared as a career catastrophe turned out to be a blessing. In his new organization, Mr. R. became known as a deal maker, divesting, acquiring, and reallocating capital. He helped to squeeze earnings from the institution, and the popular press hailed him as a financial wunderkind.

However, Mr. R.'s demeanor did not sit well with the gentlemanly culture of his new company. Most notably, Mr. R. frequently and publicly challenged the strategy of the current CEO and gave speeches to stakeholder groups on the organization's overall direction and central initiatives. These speeches, which were scheduled and composed out of his office, should have been handled by the current CEO, in whose purview they more rightfully belonged. This generated considerable internal friction, and many on the executive team believed that Mr. R., for all his talent, had crossed a sacred boundary. He found himself progressively isolated on the executive team. Knowing that the CEO position was no longer a possibility, he began a search for a new job elsewhere.

He quickly found one, this time as CEO—the job he coveted. This company (Company D) was larger still but was slow, staid, and traditional. The board wanted an outsider to shake things up a bit, to stir a little life into the institution. Mr. R. made two moves almost as soon as he stepped into his new office. First, he fired several executives who he had surmised were wedded to old practices and hired a recruiter to bring in new people from the outside. Many felt that there was no clear cause for such transitions in a short time and that the disturbances created would adversely affect operations at a critical juncture. Second, Mr. R. began negotiations to merge with another institution of equal size that together would create one of the largest companies in the United States. The product lines were complementary, and so the merger made sense, but a key part of the integration agreement was that Mr. R. would become CEO of the combined company (Company E)—which he did. The new arrangement made Mr. R. one of the highest-paid executives in any industry, and he lived lavishly, commensurate with his generous, new remuneration package.

The merger, however, did not go smoothly. First, the cultures of the two institutions were dissimilar and were never fully integrated. They were conspicuously two institutions packaged as one. Second, there were layoffs that were anathema to the institution to which Mr. R.'s company merged. They were not well received by the employees who were accustomed to hardships but previously avoided layoffs at all costs. In the past, employees accepted wage cuts, work-sharing arrangements, and other methods to avoid terminations. The institution had been run by an aging but extremely kind gentleman who considered the employees to be family and treated them as such. Third, the economic downturn hit shortly after the consummation of the deal and pounded the core businesses of the institutions especially hard. Fourth, the justification that Mr. R. provided to his board for the merger never materialized until years had passed and losses had mounted. Once the initial savings of the merger were extracted, earnings declined and costs rose precipitously. To buttress earnings, Mr. R. continued to make serial acquisitions, focusing on high-margin businesses regardless of whether the companies were adequate fits for his company or not. The company, once a tightly knit business, found itself in unfamiliar territory as a bona fide conglomerate. Fifth, Mr. R. had all executive offices resized to ones of equal size to underscore an attitude of parity. Most executives experienced shrinkage of space and considered the move a superficial and unsatisfying means of downplaying hierarchy, an issue that did not hamper communications to a significant degree in either of the merged companies before. Although Mr. R.'s office was similarly resized, his space was extended by an adjoining conference room that others did not have.

Organic growth was at a standstill, and expenses seemed out of control. Members of the board, particularly from the organization that had been merged with Mr. R.'s company, were known for their patience and thrift and were miffed that

Mr. R. seemed unwilling or unable to rein in expenses. That perception was exacerbated when the board discovered that Mr. R. wanted to build a new luxurious office tower in a more upscale part of town.

These events all transpired within a 2½-year period. Unknown to the board, as these events were unfolding, Mr. R. was negotiating a deal to join a rival and much larger international company (Company F), headquartered in the United States, as CEO. The news of the negotiations, however, was leaked to the business press, which is when the board first heard of it. The board members were understandably livid. As it happened, the deal that Mr. R. had wanted could not be accommodated by the suitor institution because of legal problems it was experiencing and other uncertain financial conditions, and therefore Company F's board did not want to commit at that time to Mr. R. and decided instead to look for an internal candidate. Once the news became public and Mr. R. was confronted by the board, he disavowed interest and sent a memorandum to the workforce where he extolled the greatness of the institution and his commitment to staying put, stating that he never had a genuine interest in leaving.

Still, in a few months' time, Mr. R. did announce to the board that he was interested in the position at Company F after all. He maintained that it was a move that he owed to his family and an obligation as father and provider. Company F, which had not found a successor inside the company and had a better understanding of its future legal exposures, had reapproached Mr. R. for the top job. As Mr. R. worked on a deal for himself with his anticipated new employer, Company E's board commenced a search for a replacement CEO. Even though the competitor institution had acceded to all Mr. R.'s demands, which were extreme (such as combining the chairman and CEO positions, which shareholders just two years previously had nixed), there were problems. The concessions made were extravagant, and the company was told by government officials that the timing of such an offer could not be worse. The economy was still in turmoil, and the president of the United States and the public blamed executive greed as a key contributing factor. There would be a public outcry, and the president would likely directly speak out against the deal, using it as an example of corporate indulgence made at the nation's expense.

With the board notably getting cold feet and members beginning to question the wisdom of their decision, the deal began to unravel. Mr. R., worried that he would be left at two altars, called the board of Company E to say that he had a change of heart and wanted to stay. The board made the expedient decision to retain Mr. R. Consequently, another dismissive memorandum was launched into the workforce, once again dispelling any interest Mr. R. had in ever wanting to leave such a wonderful organization that was so full of potential. Executives who would have been considered for the top job were not pleased to see, in their minds, a disloyal employee welcomed back into the fold, nor to have their own aspirations dashed.

Mr. R. was incredulous that both executives and board members were upset with him. Despite his public statements to the contrary—voicing that he truly wanted to stay—he thought that his desire to move should be considered entirely understandable from all perspectives: family, friends, God, and country, and all that. It was just business after all. But people were upset, and Mr. R.'s unrepentant attitude didn't help. In fact, it only increased the ire of others and further fueled interpersonal tensions.

For its part, the board wanted to see greater accountability and to receive more frequent updates from Mr. R. The company was not doing well, and Mr. R.'s unseemly diversions were perceived as costing the company money due to the chief executive's neglect. Mr. R. resented the added scrutiny, viewing it as an affront to his character and abilities. Instead of appeasing the board, Mr. R. acted belligerently and willfully passive-aggressive. He informed the board of critical happenings less frequently, feeling that the board members were unnecessarily intruding in areas outside their mandate. He failed to tell them about pending deals, layoffs, and other matters clearly within the bailiwick of the board's discretion. In addition, he was increasingly condescending toward certain executives and board members, maintaining that they had insufficient expertise and blaming them for corporate miscues. Furthermore, he asked that certain members of the board be replaced—a clear violation of protocol.

Key executives began to defect. They were irritated not only by Mr. R.'s hesitancy to consider himself a permanent member of the institution's community (as opposed to a reluctant, temporary worker who was biding his time) but also with his increasingly imperious behavior and incessant need to always be right. He had completely closed off open discourse with others, commanding and shouting orders. There was no pretense of listening. To make matters worse, Mr. R. filled vacancies by poaching talent from client organizations, which affected the company's business, since clients were clearly upset. Again, since Mr. R. conceived of his actions as only business, he couldn't fathom why the client organizations would care.

In addition, several acquired companies remained unattended, and day-to-day operations seemed to be getting further out of hand. Many of the companies that needed to be integrated felt stranded. The parent company made only cursory attempts to meld infrastructures and provided the new companies with insufficient guidance. In order to augment earnings, suspicious pricing practices within one of the larger acquired companies was permitted to continue; and while many within both the acquired and the parent company were aware of the practices and the damage they might cause to Company E's reputation and bottom line if discovered, nothing was done to discontinue their use. The practices were revealed when a whistleblower alerted government officials to them, and the parent company became the subject of several legal probes for misconduct toward clients by overcharging and shortchanging them.

Mr. R. was surprised when the board, acting in concert, requested his resignation, which he tendered.

## INTERPRETATION

The analysis of Mr. R. works backward. It begins with an overall assessment, keeping in mind that we can alter our interpretation if convincing facts can be presented that would make us see him differently. However, based on what we see from this brief description, we would render the following evaluation:

Mr. R. is ambitious and intelligent and must have adequate social skills to endear himself to those who can be of service to him. We would characterize him as indelicate with colleagues and those below him in rank, and there is little evidence that attempts were made to build a coherent team. Indeed, his repeated departures were never accompanied by fond farewells, nor did staff members ever follow him to new companies. While the welcome mat was rolled out in one place, the good riddance mat was unfolded at the other.

Overly confident to the point of arrogance, he does not like his decisions questioned, nor does he appreciate oversight. He believes that his performance will speak for itself and that opinions counter to his own are superfluous. His extravagant way of life and requests, particularly those that are clearly antithetical to existing rules or laws, suggest that he believes that he is above them—that, in his case, the rules are made to be broken and do not apply to him. This disregard of the rules likely manifested itself in different ways and made the organization susceptible to ethical malfeasance, since stretching moral boundaries to achieve results seemed an accepted cultural practice. He repeatedly undermined his sincerity and credibility among the workforce with canned, vacillating statements about staying, leaving, staying with the company, and so on. The employees would have interpreted the communications of Mr. R. as hypocritical, manipulative, and phony. There would have been watercooler jokes and jabs aplenty.

At no time does he seem aware of how others will perceive his actions, nor does effecting change through people seem particularly appealing to him. He appears to prefer the art of the deal, shedding and adding businesses based primarily on financial outcomes. His abruptness and undiplomatic encounters seemed to produce tensions wherever he went, and a lesser person with lesser skills would not have survived his abrasive demeanor for long. In the end, the companies and the people therein simply seemed to be props to further his own career. He was willing to sacrifice the friendship of allies and friends to obtain his ultimate personal goals.

How would we describe the work of this leader succinctly? He is self-absorbed, disingenuous, dispassionate, unreflective, acquisitive, imperious, egotistical, and bland. He has positive attributes, but our assessment underscores the fact that this is not a work that we would purchase. Given our overall assessment, a natural next step would be to supply our reasons and the evidence we would point to in order to support our claims. Based on our sketch, there is plenty we can say. We won't necessarily proceed in the order that our criteria are laid out in the book, but these are the criteria that we must necessarily reference in our interpretation.

Mr. R. should be taken seriously as a leader. He has proven financial acumen, and although he has done things that we would consider dumb (i.e., uncaring and thoughtless), he is not a fool.

Indeed, he has shown himself to be an adept negotiator and creative financier. We, however, would not include him as a top candidate for CEO within a traditional organization. Some organizations, such as private equity concerns where Mr. R.'s individual light would have some room to shine more brightly, might be a more appropriate fit.

Nowhere in our story does Mr. R. voice any great long-term intentions that exclude either himself as the subject or earnings as the goal. We would anticipate that neither self-interest nor making money, singly or in combination, would be particularly exhilarating to the rank and file. Mr. R. could placate higher-ups with ingenious business plans and seduce with the promise of money, absent any other reason for being in business. He certainly wasn't in business to serve clients, since he repeatedly showed disdain for them if they got in the way of his numbers or interests. He did the things that tend to keep shareholders and boards happy, until they aren't. Then, one is left without friends and a sufficient number of allies to be saved. If Mr. R. had an inkling of self-awareness, he would have felt alone in the end, because he was.

Early on, he showed that a broad strategic focus on certain business lines could be a huge corporate benefit, and he guided acquisitions and divestitures accordingly. He reallocated capital to more promising parts of the company and was wildly successful. However, that aspect of his talents seemed to have diminished with the fortunes of the most recent company. He began to pick companies based on margins rather than fit, and he wasn't paying close attention to the details of acquisitions where integration was needed in order to derive the full value from the investments. There were scant attempts to string the various units, people, processes, and systems together in order to forge a more complete and formidable entity, raising the costs to operate with dual systems, for example. Mr. R. seemed to have a fondness for financial details but not the kind of follow-through that would produce incremental benefits from his grand schemes. Additionally, we would think that given the number of transactions and comings and goings of businesses, there would have been substantial confusion and ambiguity among employees: a lack of focus regarding what the company as a whole was trying to achieve.

Putting together deals of the magnitude he did takes a lot of ingenuity and imagination. There always are people who are bigger, taller, smarter, but clearly in this arena, Mr. R. was smart and stood tall. This speaks well not only of his business mastery, but of his keen ability to foresee and overcome problems that may interfere with an agreeable solution. Unfortunately, he didn't seem to display the same flair *within* the company. The company itself looked like every other, and internal relations at the senior ranks became increasingly divisive as business deteriorated. In particular, Mr. R. increasingly berated and blamed others for many of the problems the company was experiencing. The deal maker to the external world failed to make the internal world a desirable and enriching place to be; and for several who were able to find the exit in the harsh economy, they did.

Overall, we don't see any strenuous challenge that Mr. R. was trying to conquer, no clear focus to his work, no coherence to the internal structure of the company, and no especially inspiring meaning making. Had the institution performed better, we still do not believe that Mr. R. would have worn well over time. At some point, the acquisitions would stop (or catch up with him), and something more worth working for would have to be in place. But we don't see that happening with this leader. If anything, he had almost depleted any reserve of goodwill, and his seeming tolerance for questionable business practices was producing a troublesome culture of moral permissiveness in which anything could be justified by increased margins. An organization sapped of intellectual engagement, loyalty toward the chief, a sense of community, pervasive rectitude, and a sustainable raison d'être would not have been able to withstand nor outperform competitors that had more enriching innards. In our estimation, the board's ultimate decision was the correct one to make, although we believe it should have come sooner.

---

## ASSESSING MR. R. ON THE LEADERSHIP CRITERIA

1. *What am I trying to accomplish?* In addition to his personal ambitions of leading a very large organization, Mr. R. did not appear to have any unique challenges that he was attempting to conquer. Satisfying the profit motive for companies of ever-increasing size seemed to be the stimulus behind Mr. R.'s work and ego.

2. *How will I focus, or frame, the action on what is most important without relying exclusively on words?* There is some limited evidence that the allocation of capital and the types of divestitures and acquisitions that were made were revelatory of what was most critical to the company, but Mr. R.'s methods seemed to be unidimensionally focused on financial clues. However, it does not appear that Mr. R. deployed any novel approaches that heightened excitement and that centered action on what was most critical on a daily basis.

3. *Do I have full command of the medium, methods, and techniques that will allow me to excel?* There is no question that Mr. R. grasped the finances of the industry, but he was weak on operational efficiencies and did not seem to understand or appreciate the centerpiece of organizational performance: the people.

4. *Have I assembled the various communicative devices into a coherent whole that presents a uniform message and direction?* Mr. R.'s slow responses to realignments following organizational changes made the companies seem disorderly and operationally inefficient, with inconsistent processes and systems—which, in at least one company, largely contributed to skyrocketing costs. We might also reasonably surmise that other systems, such as the reward system, were similarly out of whack and conveying contradictory values and directives.

5. *Do I use a full range of methods of communication, including symbols, to unambiguously convey my points?* There is no evidence that Mr. R. relied on richly symbolic and varied communications other than the customary written and oral communications pertaining to business conditions and metrics, mostly aimed toward stakeholder audiences.

6. *Do I produce imaginative, original, and stimulating ways of conducting business, and have I created a company where inspired thinking thrives?* There is no indication that Mr. R. used alluring, enterprising techniques to make critical points, capture people's imaginations, and instill original thinking and action. It all appears to be straightforward business as usual.

7. *Do I act in a manner that is true to my beliefs and that clearly articulates who I am and what I stand for?* Mr. R. comes across as self-interested, and his hollow attempts to atone for his touting a great organization that he wished to leave clearly would have been viewed as insincere and inauthentic.

8. *Do I produce a challenging and intellectually stimulating environment where people feel compelled*

*to take on issues and work hard to generate solutions?*
We would surmise that Mr. R. pushed members of
the accounting and finance departments particularly
regarding due diligence on deals, but we see little in
his behavior where he tried to enlarge the circle of
engagement and involve more people in the intricacies
of the enterprise and its success.

9.  *Do I produce an enriching and satisfying environment
    where people are able to thrive and grow?* We cannot
    think of anything exceptional in Mr. R.'s history in
    which he strived to make the departments, functions,
    and companies he headed uniquely pleasurable and
    exhilarating places to work. Any pleasure there is to
    be found would have had to come from work done
    with respected colleagues or from the job itself, rather
    than from what Mr. R. provided through his role
    independently—meaning there is a good chance that
    most employees could find the same satisfactions
    elsewhere if there were jobs to be had and they bothered
    to look. Indeed, development was never a priority for
    Mr. R.'s own immediate staff.

10. *Am I able to build a community that is cemented by
    basic human needs and concerns?* To us, an impostor
    is someone who feigns belonging to a group that he
    really considers himself outside of. That sums up
    our understanding of Mr. R. He never felt a part of
    the organizations to which he avowed support. It is
    like a person telling an off-color joke that a particular
    community of people will like but that the teller herself
    finds offensive—it is a joke told to a community that
    the teller doesn't feel affiliated with. That is how we see
    Mr. R.—standing outside the perimeter of a circle that
    contains everyone else.

11. *Do I manifest a distinctive management style, and am I able to adapt my style and approach in order to fit the conditions in which I am operating?* If anything, Mr. R. became stylistically less adaptive as business pressures rose and more demands were placed upon him. Because Mr. R. was accustomed to being self-reliant and doing things his way, the threat of increased accountability was antithetical to his usual modus operandi, and it ignited a backlash of extreme independence. Rather than changing to adapt to the circumstances, he behaved in a way that exacerbated problems with the board and fellow executives. His actions were contextually out of place and unhelpful, and he appeared incapable of changing.

12. *Am I worthy of being judged and appreciated as a leader?* Worthy, yes. There is nothing radically outside of normal human behavior and business fashion that should prohibit an evaluation of Mr. R.'s leadership acumen. Whatever else Mr. R. might be, his position as a leader and his subsequent decisions need to be taken seriously.

Despite the fact that Mr. R. was personally successful and in high demand in the executive marketplace, we don't find his leadership abilities to be particularly impressive. Although we think that this example presents an argument to hire a strong number two person to oversee operations and work alongside Mr. R., we suspect that an arrangement approximate to co-CEOs would not work given Mr. R.'s ambitions and reluctance to accept guidance from others.

In summary, we hope that we have appropriately illustrated the complexities and necessities of interpreting the quality of leadership—and that it is understood that when we say someone is a great leader, we mean more than he or she had a good year.

# Notes

## Introduction

1. The argument we make is known as *cluster theory* in the arts, which defines works of art as having a set of attributes. The set we provide is unique, but we have used different sources for guidance, taking various lists of criteria and compiling them into one that we believe satisfies conditions for art and leadership. These lists appear in R. L. Anderson, *Calliope's Sisters: A Comparative Study of Philosophies of Art*, Upper Saddle River, NJ: Prentice-Hall, 1990; E. J. Bond, "The Essential Nature of Art," *American Philosophical Quarterly*, vol. 12, 1975, pp. 177–183; D. Dutton, "A Naturalist Definition of Art," *The Journal of Aesthetics and Art Criticism*, vol. 64, 2006, pp. 367–377; and B. Gaut, "The Cluster Account of Art Defended," *British Journal of Aesthetics*, vol. 45, 2005, pp. 273–288.

2. W. Baker and M. O'Malley, *Leading with Kindness: How Good People Consistently Get Superior Results*, New York: AMACOM, 2008.

## Chapter 2

1. A nice history of what it meant to stage a scene is presented in R. Shusterman, "Art as Dramatization," *The Journal of Aesthetics and Art Criticism*, vol. 59, 2001, pp. 363–372.

2. The importance of frames to artists, including the examples we report here, are from B. E. Savedoff, "Frames," *The Journal of Aesthetics and Art Criticism*, vol. 57, 1990, pp. 345–356.

3. A. Bryant, "Making Sure That Ideas Are Employee Owned," *New York Times*, January 22, 2012, p. BU2.

## Chapter 3

1. J. S. Lubin and D. Cimilluca, "Fighting to Retake Top Job," *Wall Street Journal*, December 13, 2011, p. B1.

# CHAPTER 4

1. S. Greenhouse, "U.S. Mail May Arrive a Bit Later," *New York Times*, December 6, 2011, p. B1.

# CHAPTER 5

1. Since all art involves representation, finding something a little different is hard to come by. Thankfully, we encountered the wonderful piece on rain cited here which provides the example and informs our discussion: B. Sandrisser, "Rain," in Philip Alperson, ed., *The Philosophy of the Visual Arts,* New York: Oxford University Press, 1992.

2. For a succinct, illuminating discussion of improvisation in music, see C. S. Gould and K. Keaton, "The Essential Role of Improvisation in Musical Performance," *The Journal of Aesthetics and Art Criticism*, vol. 58, 2000, pp. 143–148.

# CHAPTER 6

1. V. Woolf, *Mrs. Dalloway,* New York: Harcourt, 1925.

2. Reported in F. Sparshott, "Imagination—the Very Idea," *The Journal of Aesthetics and Art Criticism*, vol. 48, 1990, pp. 1–8.

3. J. Bussey, "The Anti-Kodak: How a U.S. Firm Innovates and Thrives," *Wall Street Journal,* January, 13, 2012, p. B1.

# CHAPTER 7

1. This example comes from C. Korsmeyer, "Aesthetic Deception: On Encounters with the Past," *The Journal of Aesthetics and Art Criticism*, vol. 66, 2008, pp. 117–127.

# CHAPTER 8

1. A. Bryant, "All Are Welcome at His Meetings," *New York Times*, March 20, 2011, p. BU2.

2. M. Lynn, "The Fallen King of Finland," *Bloomberg Businessweek*, September 20–26, 2011, pp. 7–8.

3. K. Berman and J. Knight, "What Your Employees Don't Know Will Hurt You," *Wall Street Journal*, February 27, 2012, p. R4.

## CHAPTER 9

1. M. Beardsley, *The Aesthetic Point of View*, Ithaca, NY: Cornell University Press, 1982.

2. W. Spiegelman, "Space Oddities," *Bloomberg Businessweek*, February 13, 2012, p. 78.

3. A. Bryant, "WET Design and the Improv Approach to Listening," *New York Times*, April 20, 2011, p. BU2.

4. The idea of aesthetic health and artist dropouts comes from K. Melchionne, "Artistic Dropouts," in Carolyn Korsmeyer, ed., *Aesthetics: The Big Questions*, Malden, MA: Blackwell Publishers, 1998.

5. H. Melville, *Bartleby, the Scrivener: A Story of Wall Street*, Lexington: Create Space.

## CHAPTER 10

1. A rich discussion of the adaptive role of art in dispensing shared understandings can be found in N. Carroll, "Art and Human Nature," *The Journal of Aesthetics and Art Criticism*, vol. 62, 2004, pp. 95–107.

2. C. Da Fonseca-Wollhein, "Qawwali Ambassadors," *Wall Street Journal*, October 26, 2011, p. D5.

3. E. Press, *Beautiful Souls: Saying No, Breaking Ranks, and Heeding the Voice of Conscience in Dark Times*, New York: Farrar, Strauss & Giroux, 2012.

## CHAPTER 14

1. See W. G. Bennis and J. O'Toole, "How Business Schools Lost Their Way," *Harvard Business Review*, May 2005, pp. 96–104; and H. Mintzberg, *Managers Not MBAs: A Hard Look at the Soft Practice of Managing and Management Development*, San Francisco: Berrett-Koehler, 2005.

2. J. Canals, "In Search of a Greater Impact: New Corporate and Social Challenges for Business Schools," in J. Canals, ed., *The Future of Leadership Development: Corporate Needs and the Role of Business Schools*, New York: Palgrave Macmillan, 2011.

3. M. Gentile, *Giving Voice to Values: How to Speak Your Mind When You Know What's Right*, New Haven, CT: Yale University Press, 2012.

4. W. D. Cohan, "Guess Who Wins," *Bloomberg Businessweek*, March 19, 2012, pp. 16–17.

# Index

# About the Authors

**Michael O'Malley, PhD,** has consulted with the world's largest organizations on matters related to leadership and human resource management for more than 30 years. He previously served as the executive editor for business, economics, and law at Yale University Press.

**William F. Baker, PhD,** directs the Bernard I. Schwartz Center for Media Education and Public Policy at Fordham University. He has won seven Emmys for his work in broadcasting.